Introducing Auguste Rodin

Pippa Stephenson-Sit

The Burrell
COLLECTION

First published in 2022 by Glasgow Museums Publishing.
Text © Culture and Sport Glasgow (Museums) 2022.
Images © CSG CIC Glasgow Museums Collection, unless otherwise acknowledged.

ISBN 978-1-908638-36-6

Written by Pippa Stephenson-Sit
Edited by Kim Teo
Designed by John Westwell
Photography by Maureen Kinnear and Iona Shepherd

Images supplied by Glasgow Museums Photo Library
www.csgimages.org.uk
www.glasgowmuseums.com

Front cover image: detail from *The Age of Bronze*, 1875–77, 7.18
Back cover image: *The Man with the Broken Nose*, about 1863–64, 7.10

Acknowledgements

All efforts have been made to trace copyright holders, but if any omissions have been made inadvertently, please contact the publishers.

Image credits: © Agence Photographique du musée Rodin – photo Jerome Manoukian: 18, 43, 63; Bridgeman images: p. 17 (right), p. 25 (right), 61, 62 (left); © John Bethell/Bridgeman Images: 65; © Musée Rodin: p. 8, p. 17 (left), 30, 31, 40, 44, 57, 58; © Musée Rodin (photo Christian Baraja): p. 39 (left and right); © National Portrait Gallery, London: p. 6; © Nicolò Orsi Battaglini/Bridgeman Images; p. 25 (left).

We are very grateful to Northwestern University Press for kind permission to include, on p. 33: Excerpt lines 487–500 from *The Testament* by François Villon, from *Poems.* Translated by David Georgi, Evanston: Northwestern University Press, 2013, p. 61. (© 2013 by David Georgi. Published 2013 by Northwestern University Press. All rights reserved.)

Printed in Scotland by J Thomson Colour Printers, Glasgow
Cover printed on 350gsm Galerie Satin; text printed on 150gsm Galerie Satin

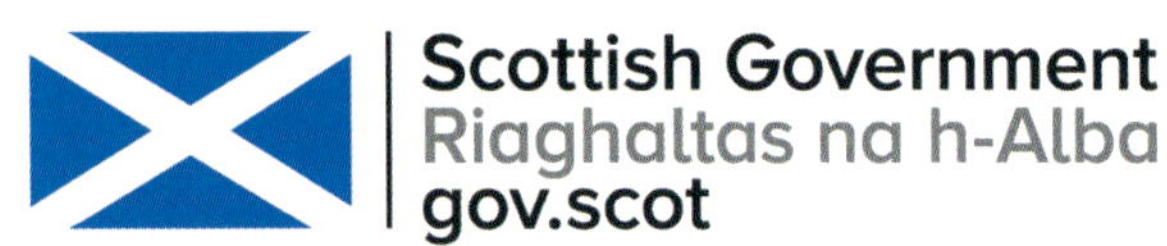

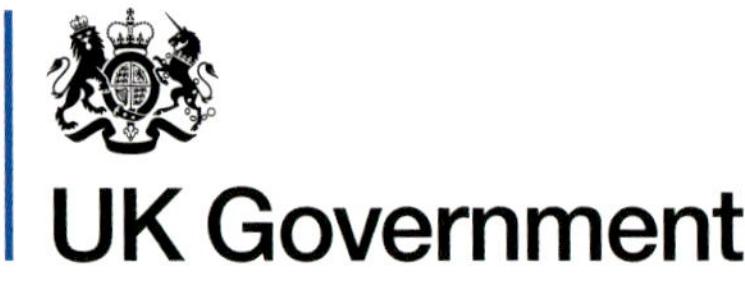

Contents

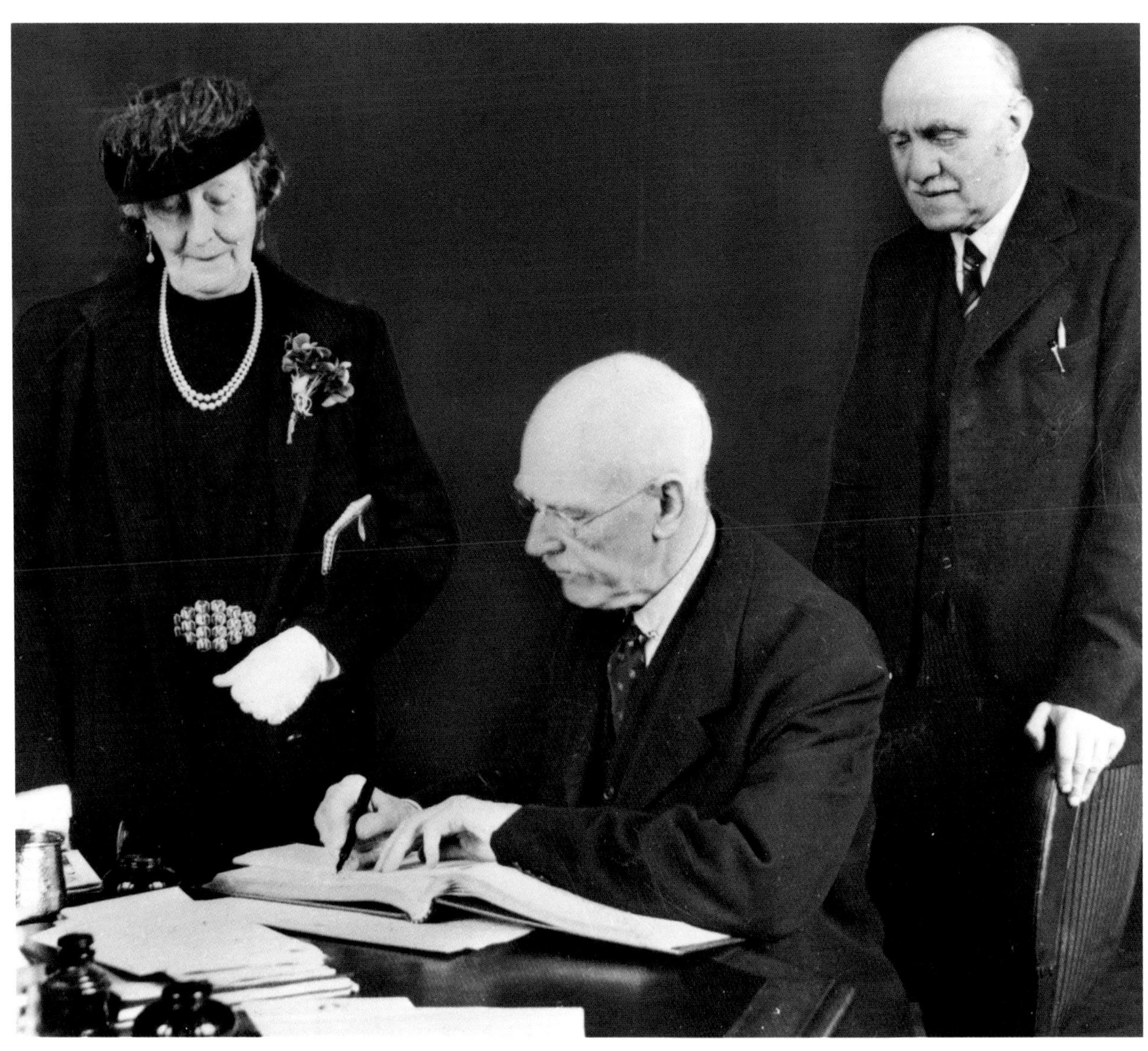

Sir William Burrell (seated), Constance, Lady Burrell and
Lord Provost James Welsh at the City Chambers, Glasgow,
1944, on the occasion of Sir William receiving the Freedom
of the City of Glasgow. Glasgow Museums Archive,
GMA.2013.1.1.470.

The Burrell Collection: The Gift of Sir William and Constance, Lady Burrell

The Burrell Collection comprises over 9,000 objects gifted to the city of Glasgow by Sir William Burrell (1861–1958) and his wife Constance, Lady Burrell (1875–1961). The main gift, of around 6,000 objects, was in 1944, but Burrell continued to add to it until his death, and the Collection has been further augmented with funds gifted by Burrell and administered by the Burrell Trustees.

Sir William made his fortune in shipping at a time when Glasgow was second city of the Empire. Collecting was a lifelong passion, and his treasures adorned his various homes: archive photographs show tapestries, sculpture, paintings and furniture in his house in Great Western Terrace, Glasgow. These, and also ceramics, stained glass, arms and armour and textiles, were displayed at Hutton Castle, his home in the Scottish Borders.

A sophisticated collector with a discerning eye, Burrell appreciated fine craftsmanship and meticulous attention to detail. From tapestries to sculpture, nineteenth-century French art to Chinese bronzes, medieval stained glass to Islamic carpets, the breadth and quality of his collection demonstrate his wide-ranging embrace of different cultures and art forms. Sir William also gave money for a new building to house his collection, and it is now displayed in a purpose-built museum in the centre of Pollok Country Park, on the south side of Glasgow. The park was gifted to the city in 1967 by Mrs Anne Maxwell Macdonald (1906–2011), and a competition, sponsored by the Royal Institute of British Architects, was held to design a suitable building within it to house the Collection. The winners of the competition, architects Barry Gasson, John Meunier and Brit Andresen, came up with a building which not only displays the Collection to advantage, but is also in harmony with the surrounding parkland. The building opened in 1983, but through the decades the Scottish weather took its toll and in 2016 the Category-A listed building closed for an ambitious programme of refurbishment, redisplay and reinterpretation.

This series is designed to introduce different parts of the Collection. Written by subject specialists, each book gives an insight into the Burrell's treasures. We, the Trustees of The Burrell Collection, are delighted to see the amount of new research that has been carried out on the objects in the collection, and hope that visitors will continue to enjoy Sir William and Constance, Lady Burrell's gift for many generations to come.

Professor Frances Fowle
Senior Trustee, Sir William Burrell's Trust

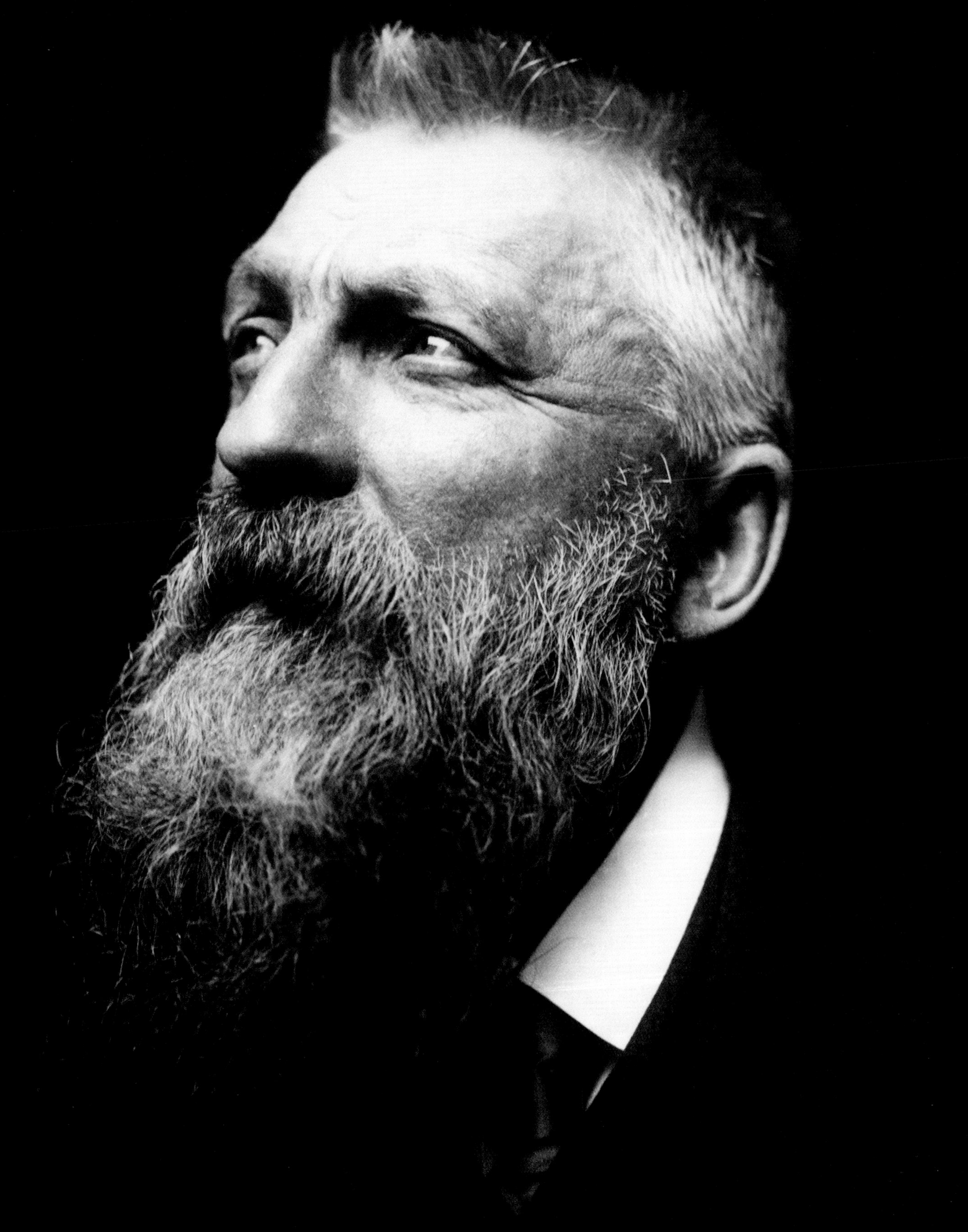

Introduction

The sculptures of Auguste Rodin (1840–1917) can be found across the globe, whether grand monuments in busy cities, or artworks in collections both private and public. Among these are some of the world's most famous sculptures, including *The Kiss* and *The Thinker.*

Rodin is often referred to as 'the Father of Modern Sculpture'. The key to the artist's modernity lies in his complete fidelity to nature. Rodin wanted to show life and truth through his art. In his words, 'I obey Nature in everything, and I never pretend to command her. My only ambition is to be servilely faithful to her.' But it was not enough to simply reproduce a subject's appearance: Rodin's sculptures reveal feelings and personality. They were based on the faces and bodies of real people, regardless of their age, size or physical imperfections.

The way Rodin worked was unconventional and exciting. When he modelled clay, or instructed craftsmen how to sculpt his designs into marble, he liked to leave evidence of how the material had been worked. In many of his sculptures we can see where he twisted and pulled, or imprinted deeply into the clay. This allows us a direct connection with the artist, imagining the moment he shaped the wet clay in front of him.

William Burrell was an early collector of Rodin. By 1901 he owned at least one sculpture by the artist and continued to collect examples until the late 1930s. He lived alongside the artwork, displaying at least one sculpture in his home. By the time he and his wife, Constance, Lady Burrell gifted much of their collection to the city of Glasgow in 1944, Burrell had amassed 14 Rodins. This gives the Burrell Collection the second largest group of works by Rodin in the United Kingdom.

Britain was quick to embrace the work of Rodin, with sculptures entering private collections from the early 1890s. Alexander Reid (1854–1928), a Scottish art dealer with a gallery in Glasgow, was the first to sell the work of Rodin in the United Kingdom. Reid had a reputation for supplying Scotland with fresh, modern French art, and was buying sculptures directly from Rodin as early as 1892. Burrell is known to have owned a Rodin as early as 1901, when he lent a piece called *Maternal Love* to the Glasgow International Exhibition, and it is likely that he acquired this and other works through Reid. Glasgow was the first British city to buy a work by Rodin for its public collection, purchasing *Bust of Victor Hugo* from Glasgow's International Exhibition of 1888. The city had a special appreciation for Rodin: as well as being asked to contribute to exhibitions in 1892 and 1893, he was given an honorary doctorate from the University of Glasgow in 1906.

William Burrell's sustained collecting indicates the variety of Rodin's oeuvre, from intimate sculptural groups to striking life-size figures. As Sir William could clearly appreciate, there is nothing quite like standing in front of a Rodin. The pure power of human emotion, expressed through lifelike faces, and bodies so real you could imagine them stepping from the plinth, leave Rodin's reputation as the 'Father of Modern Sculpture' standing firm.

With his full beard, closely cropped hair and piercing blue eyes, Rodin's appearance left a memorable impression. Auguste Rodin, 1902, by George Charles Beresford. National Portrait Gallery, London, NPG x6573.

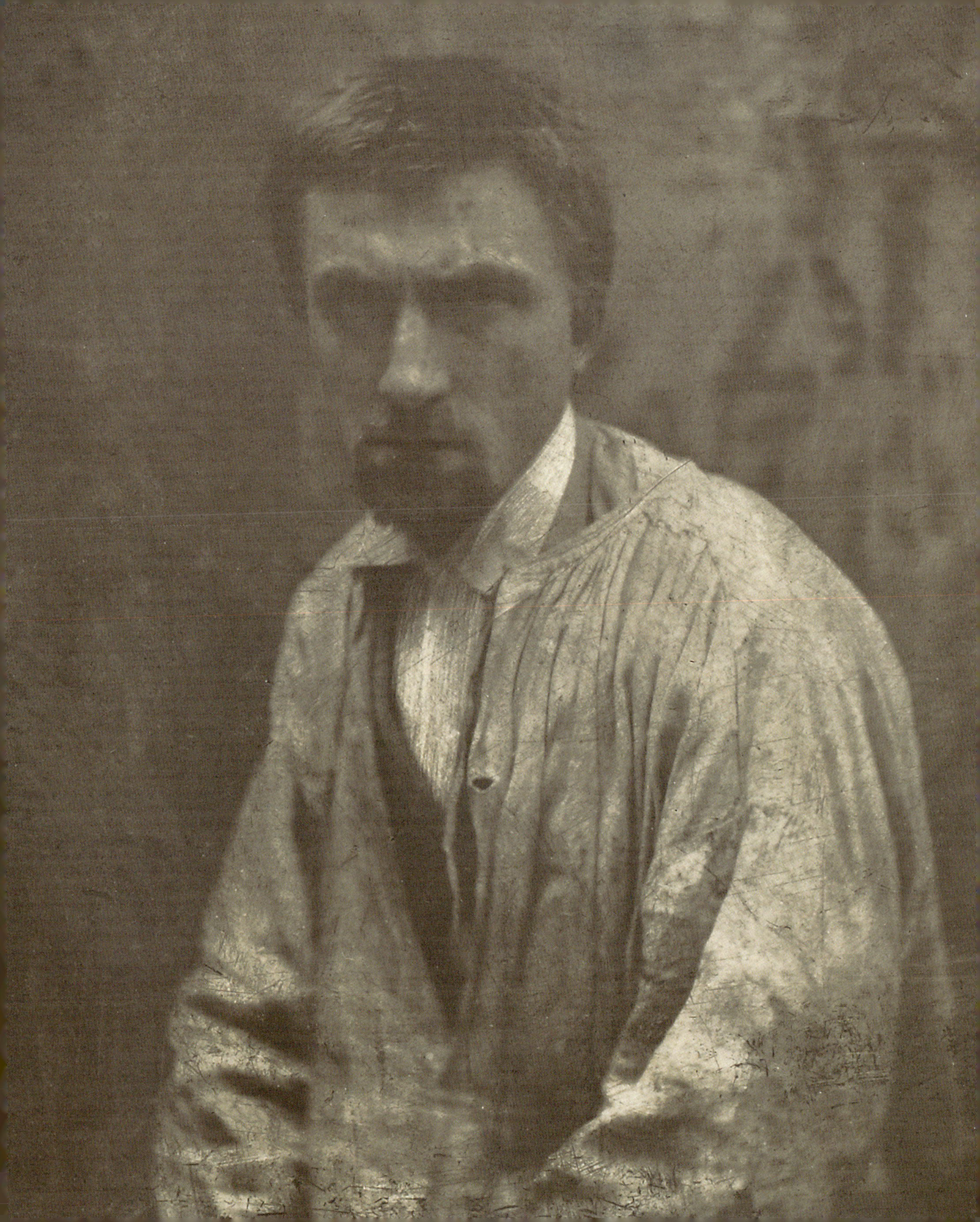

Early Rodin

Although he later became one of history's most famous sculptors, Rodin's early years were a struggle. The son of a clerk in a police department, Rodin grew up in Paris on the edge of poverty. Sadly, he lost two of his siblings when he was young; the death of his beloved older sister Maria (1837–62) when he was aged 22 had a particularly profound impact upon him.

Rodin showed a precocious talent for drawing, and in 1854 joined the École Impériale Spéciale de Dessin et de Mathématiques, known as the 'Petit École', a school designed to prepare the next generation of industrial workers, such as goldsmiths and textile craftsmen. For those wanting to become an artist, the next step was to enrol in the school of fine art, the École des Beaux-Arts. Rodin tried and failed to be accepted three years in a row – although his drawings fulfilled requirements, he did not pass the sculpting assessment. Being rejected from the École set Rodin on an unconventional route to becoming an artist. Without this institutional support Rodin had to find his own way, working for 20 years in the studios of other artists before he was successful enough to concentrate solely on his own art. He accepted jobs in ceramic studios, where he made vases and ornaments, and fulfilled other artists' designs for public monuments or decorative schemes for buildings. Missing out on a place at the École also meant that it was difficult for Rodin to have a work accepted at the Salon, Paris's

annual exhibition of art where all new artists were expected to be shown. It was not until 1878 that Rodin finally had a work, *The Man with the Broken Nose*, accepted there. Around that time, his sculptures started to get noticed. However, this attention was not always for the reasons he had hoped. The artist was falsely accused of casting his 1875 sculpture *The Age of Bronze* directly from the body of a model, rather than sculpting it based on observation (see pp. 14–17).

Although they must have been difficult and frustrating times for the emerging artist, it was thanks to his early years that Rodin built a strong artistic training, mastering a diversity of mediums from pottery to stone and marble. In his words, 'I began as an artisan to become an artist.' Those years also gave him experience of working in a large, productive artist's studio, which would come in useful when he set up his own in later years. Furthermore, working to other people's designs gave him a strong focus during the times he could develop his own art. He worked on his sculpture in the evenings and weekends in a rented studio, as well as visiting the Louvre museum to study classical sculptures.

When this photograph was taken, Rodin was struggling to come to terms with the death of his sister Maria. His father's health was failing, and he had been repeatedly rejected from art school, the École des Beaux-Arts. Auguste Rodin in a sculptor's smock, about 1862, by Charles Aubry. Musée Rodin, Paris, Ph.4.

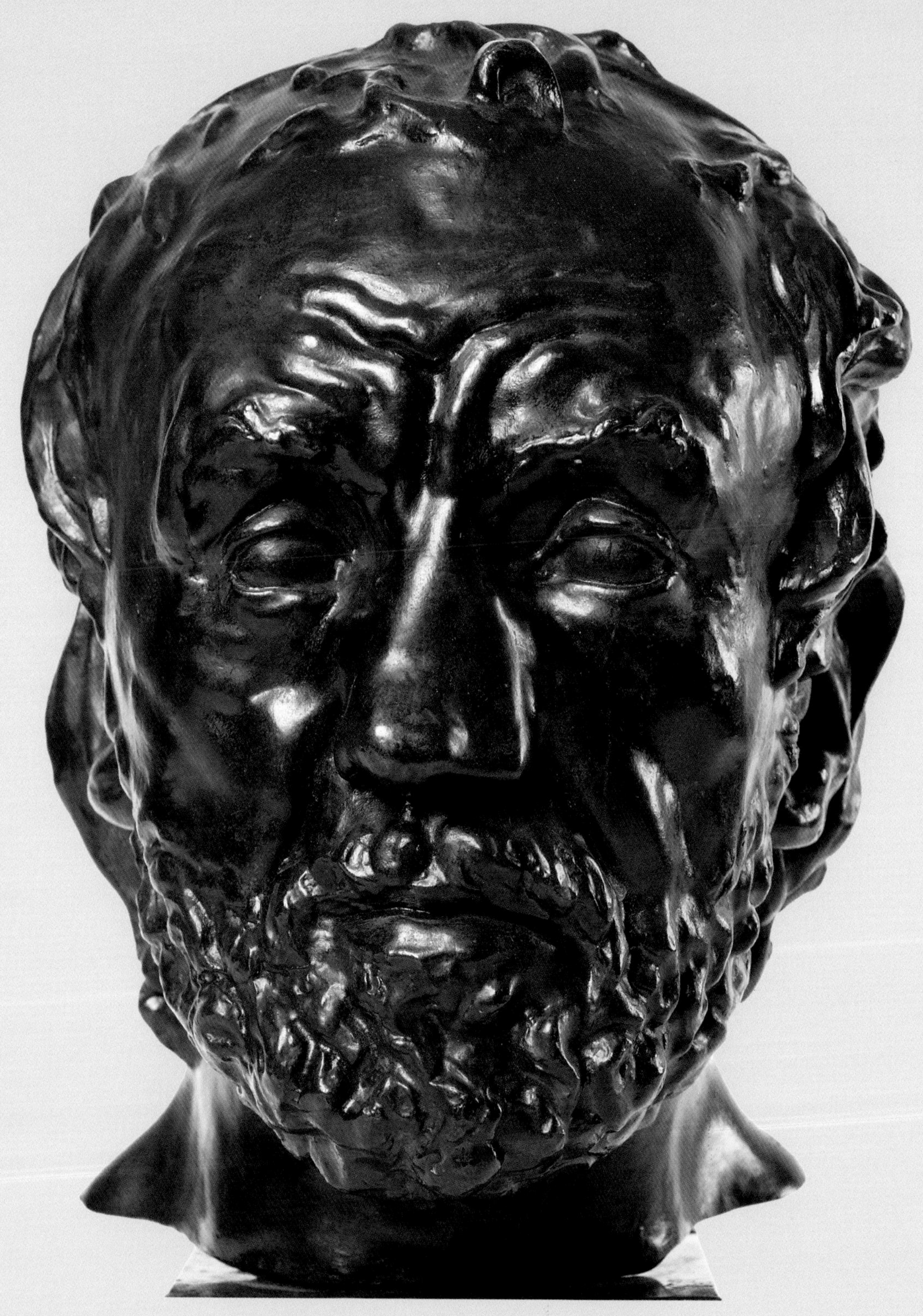

Sculpture in Focus

The Man with the Broken Nose, 1863–64
Cast in bronze by Alexis Rudier Foundry, before 1930
Bronze
26 x 18.9 x 22 cm
7.10

Rodin based what he would later refer to as his 'first great sculpture' on the weather-beaten face of a local workman, named Bibi, who had a prominent broken nose. Rodin recognized Greek ancestry in Bibi, an attractive trait to the artist, who had been carefully studying classical Ancient Greek sculpture in the nearby Louvre. The face is styled in a way to emulate the masks and busts he would have seen in that foremost Parisian art museum. However, those faces belonged to philosophers, rulers or ancient gods, not a lowly workman. By modelling the face on a real, everyday man, but in the style normally reserved for gods and the great, he created something that was classical and yet at the same time incredibly modern.

When Rodin was making this sculpture he was working in a cold studio. During winter the clay sculpture froze, causing a chunk to break from the back of the head. Rodin cast it anyway and submitted the artwork to the 1865 Paris Salon. The jury did not know what to make of the sculpture, which was cut abruptly at the neck, rather than showing the shoulders as was more usual in traditional busts. The classical appearance, which was different to what other sculptors of the time were doing, along with the missing piece at the back of the head, were further elements that made this a highly unusual and somewhat confusing piece. It was promptly rejected. Nevertheless, Rodin did not forget this important work, which 13 years later he successfully resubmitted to the Salon, and about which he stated, 'I have kept that mask before my mind in everything I have done.'

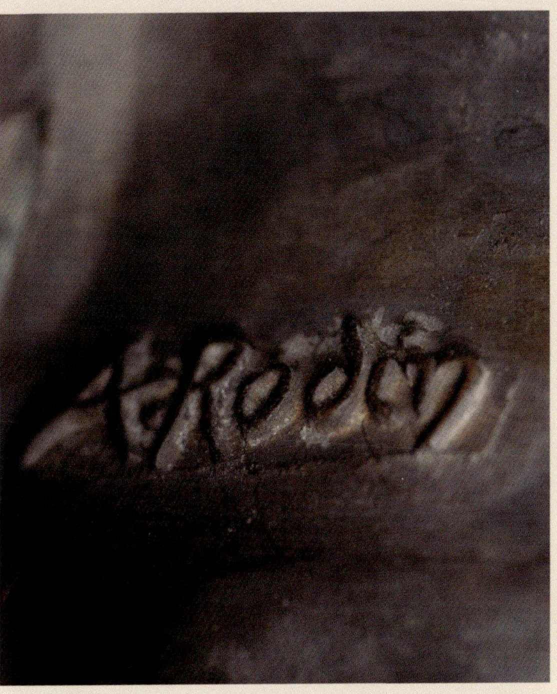

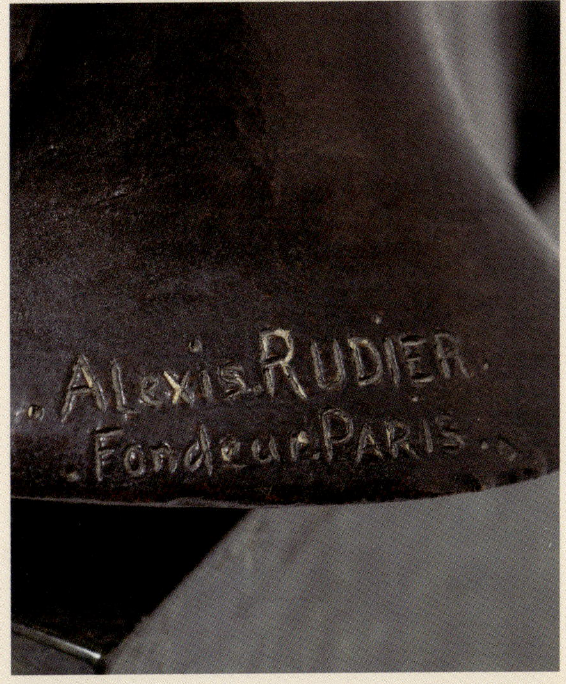

Above right and right: The artist's signature is on the side of the sculpture, towards the back. On the other side are the words 'Alexis RUDIER Fondeur PARIS', used to mark casts produced at the Alexis Rudier Foundry.

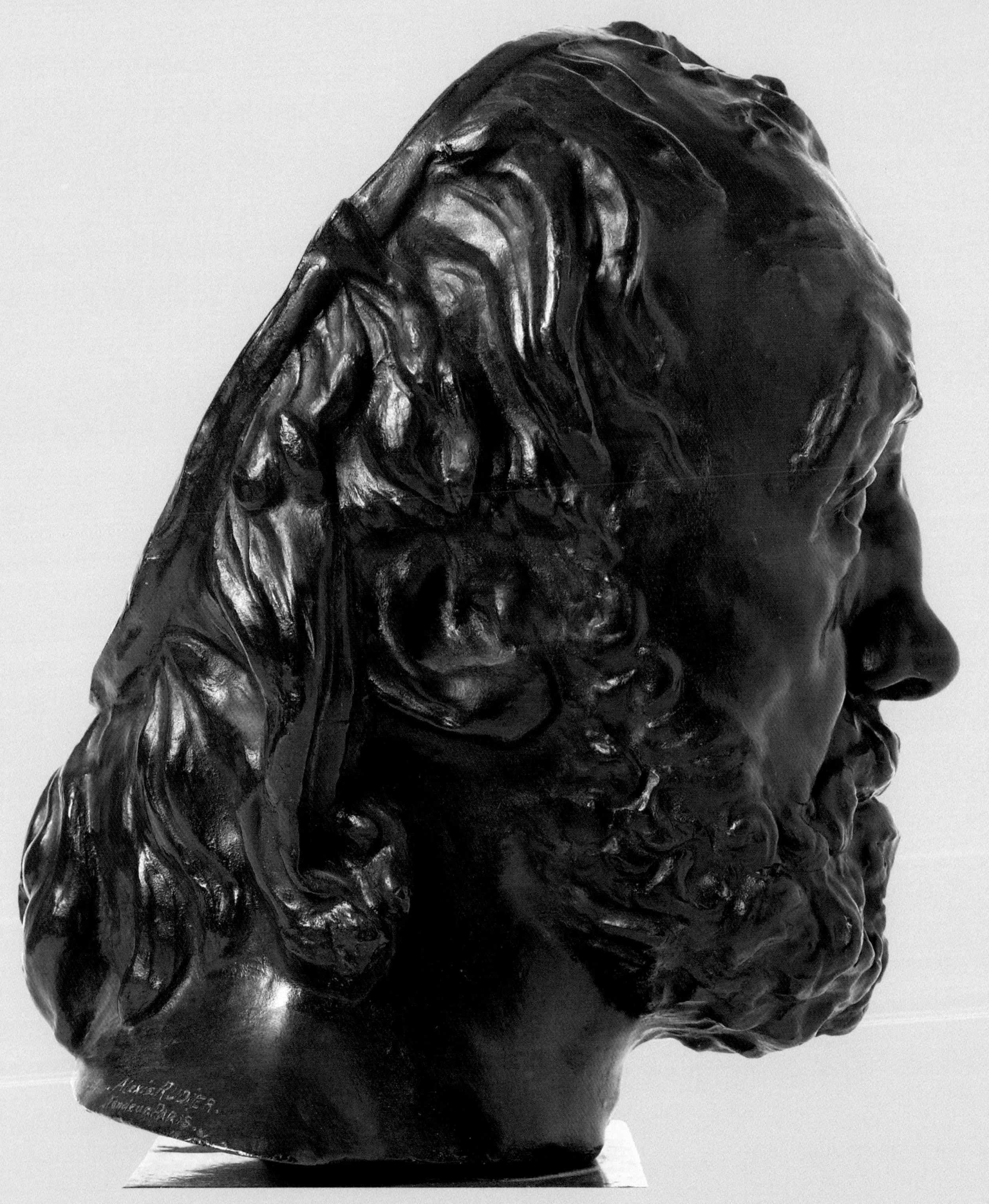

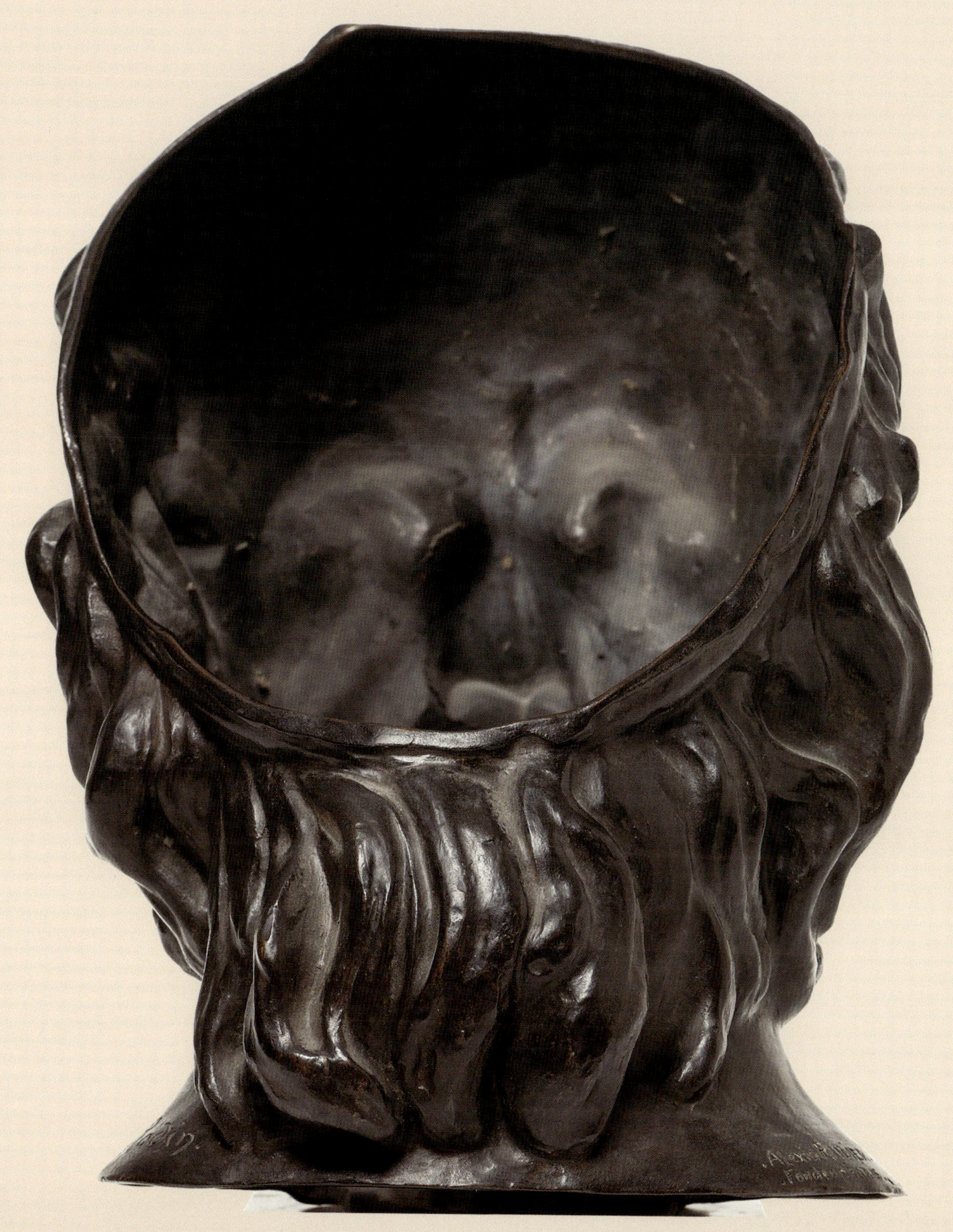

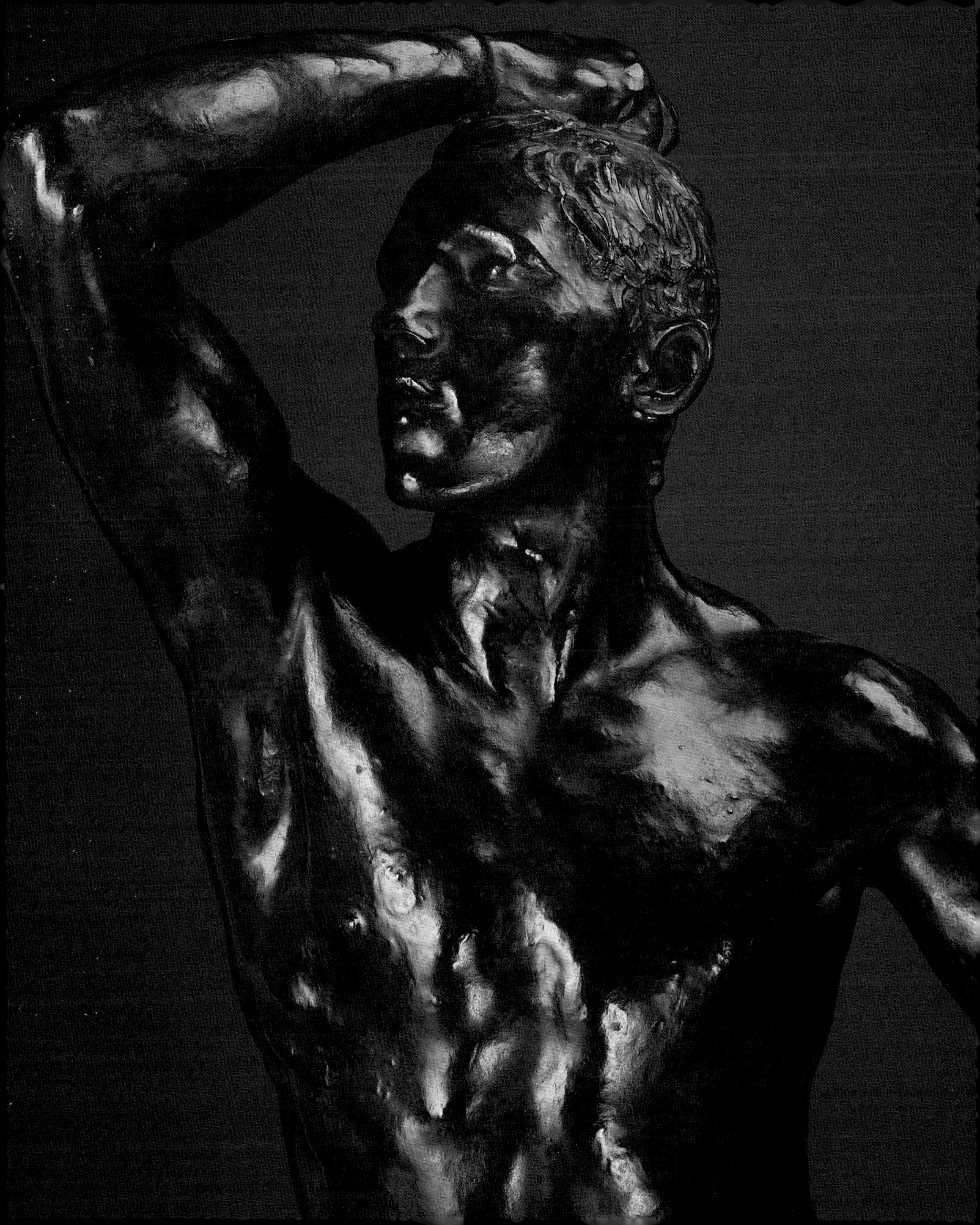

The Age of Bronze, 1875–77

Cast in bronze by Alexis Rudier Foundry, before 1937
Bronze
183.5 x 68.5 x 57 cm
7.18

For 18 months whilst living in Belgium, Rodin worked on what was to be his first surviving life-size human figure. The result is a smoothly finished sculpture with a classical appeal. This early style is quite different from the roughly hewn, distressed surface Rodin became known for in later years.

A local soldier, Auguste Neyt (b. 1853), was the model for the figure. To achieve such anatomically perfect proportions, Rodin viewed Neyt from every angle, including from above by standing on a ladder, making sure that the figure was completely correct in its modelling. Rodin did such a good job, however, that when it was exhibited in 1877, first in Brussels and later that year in Paris, the figure was dismissed as being made directly from the body, akin to a plaster cast, rather than a sculpture based on 18 months of painstaking observation. The accusations hugely frustrated Rodin. He asked friends, including the engraver Gustave Biot (1833–1905), to make public statements declaring the work to be based on observation, and he wrote a lengthy letter imploring the French Ministry of Fine Arts to rethink their position. It was only after a group of artists, including the esteemed sculptors Alfred Boucher (1850–1934) and Paul Dubois (1829–1905), lobbied the Ministry that Rodin's *The Age of Bronze* was understood to be a work of originality and skill, with a cast bought by the state in 1880.

Rodin seems to have grappled with the title and interpretation of his sculpture. He originally imagined the man holding a spear in his left hand. However, he chose to omit this detail, so the sculpture would not be connected with anything specific. He first exhibited the sculpture with the title *The Conquered Man*. Critics were confused by the man's expression: were his closed eyes and open mouth indicating death? Perhaps even suicide? Rodin quickly

changed the title to its current one, moving away from such a narrow, narrative interpretation. The title Rodin chose, *The Age of Bronze*, makes reference to the third of the five ages of mankind as described by the Ancient Greek poet Hesiod. The Bronze Age is characterized by man's ability to make objects out of bronze, including wartime weapons. The figure seems to be awakening to this new age, as if from slumber, his eyes opening and arms stretching. Rodin explained that he wanted to show 'one of the first inhabitants of our world, physically perfect, but in the infancy of comprehension, and beginning to awake to the world's meaning.'

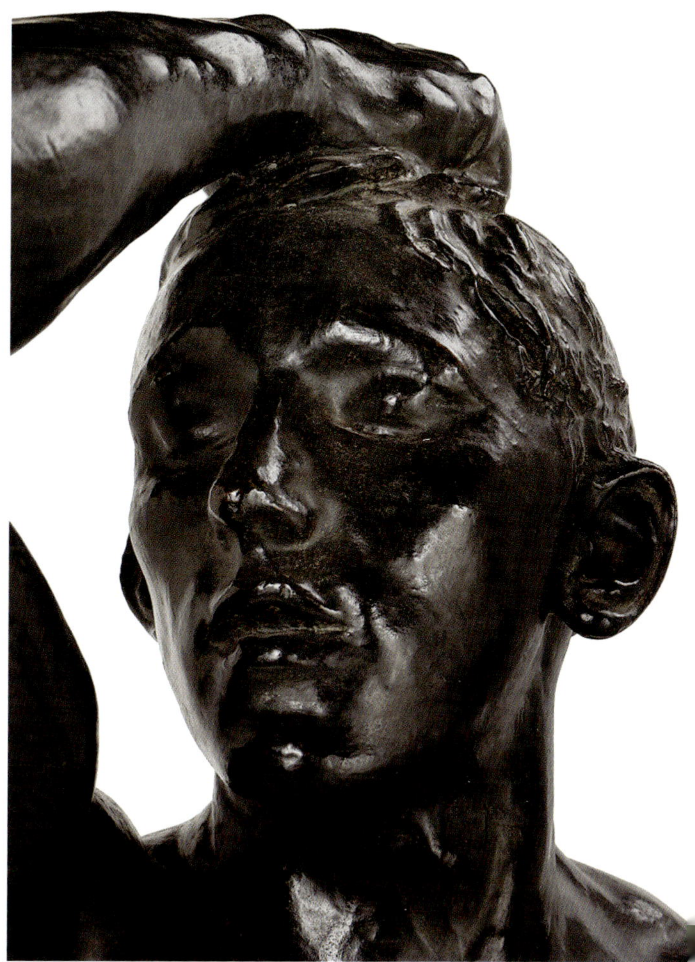

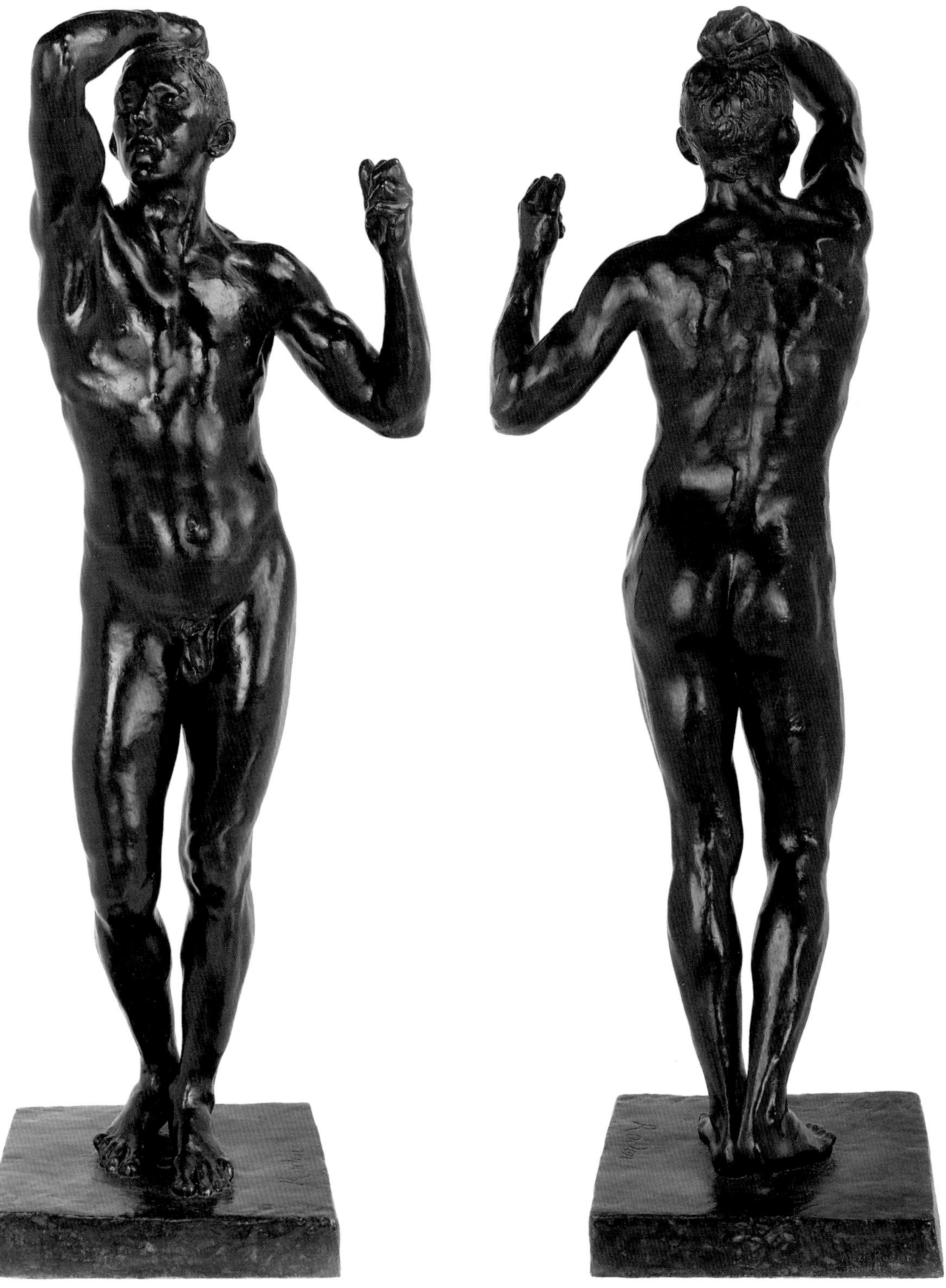

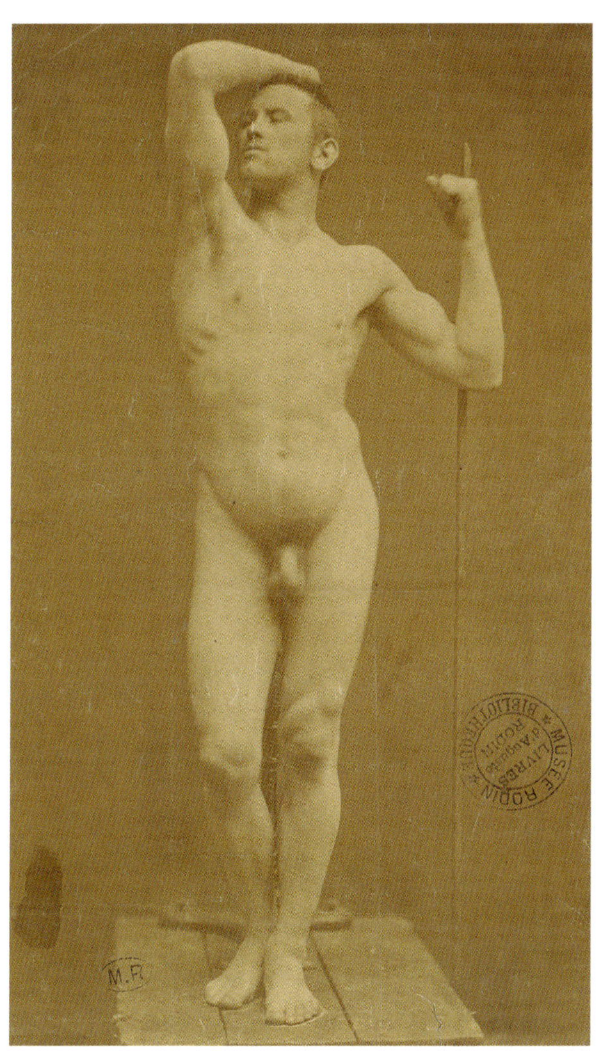

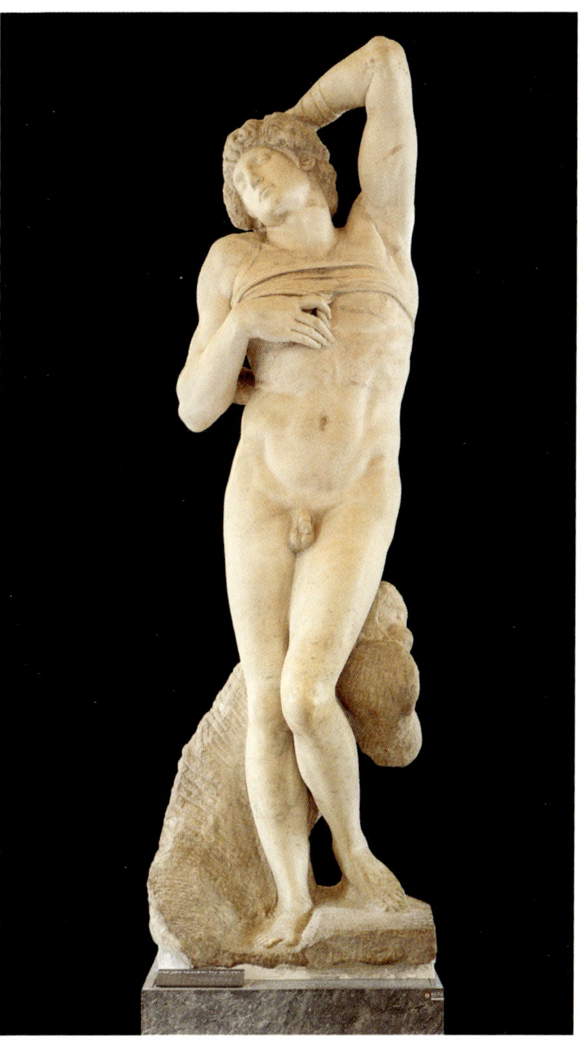

A 22-year-old Belgian soldier, Auguste Neyt, modelled for Rodin's life-size sculpture *The Age of Bronze*. His natural way of posing appealed to Rodin more than the conventional poses of professional models. Auguste Neyt, 1877, by Gaudenzio Marconi. Musée Rodin, Paris, Ph.270.

The Italian artist Michelangelo Buonarroti greatly influenced Rodin. The distinctive pose of *The Dying Slave*, with his elbow raised, is mirrored by Rodin's *The Age of Bronze*. *Captive*, known as *The Dying Slave*, 1513–15, by Michelangelo, marble. The Louvre, Paris, MR 1590.

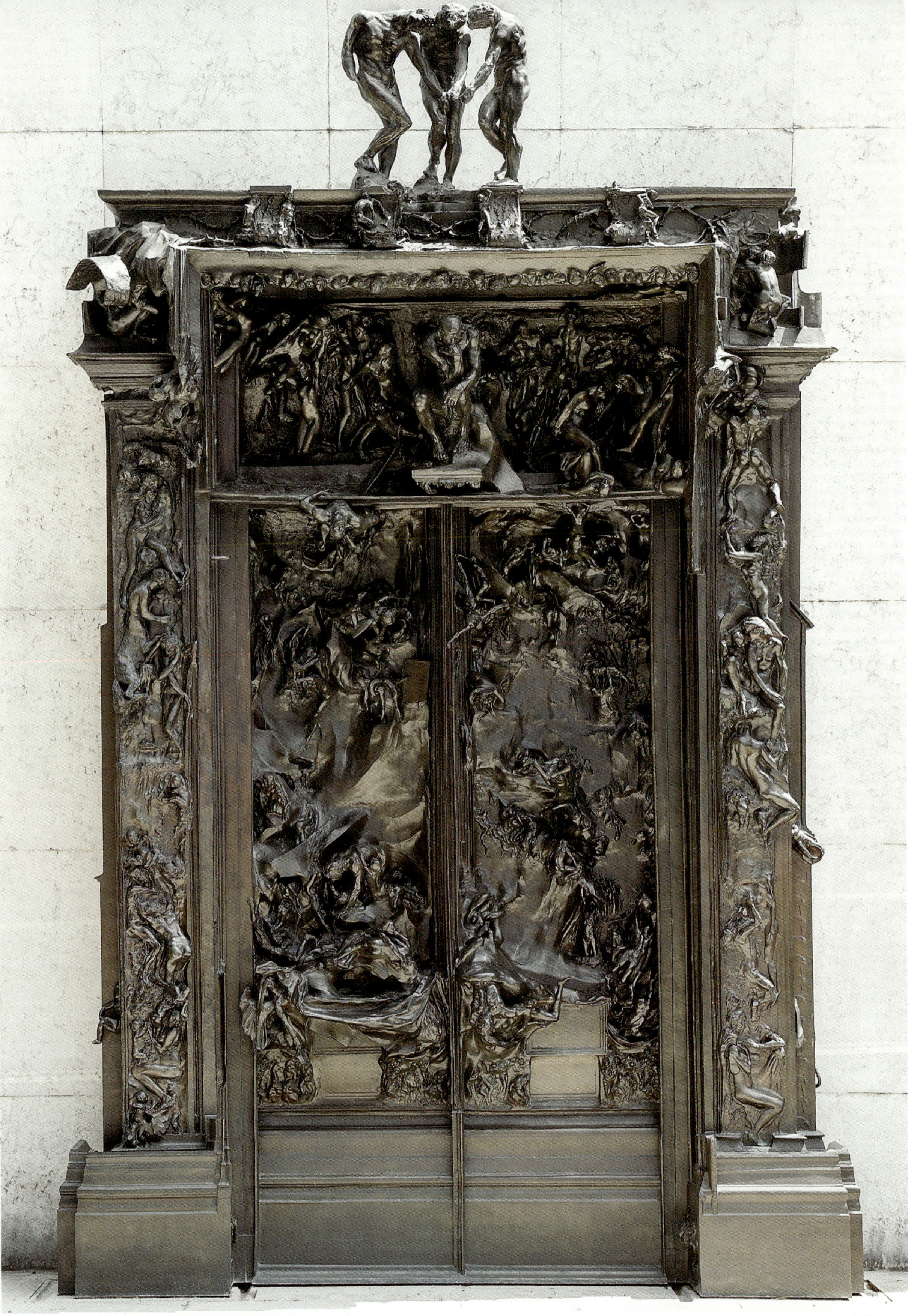

The Gates of Hell

In 1880 Rodin received a commission which was to change his life. The artist was tasked by the French Ministry of Fine Arts with creating bronze doors for a new decorative arts museum to be opened in Paris, the Musée des Arts Décoratifs. Although the building was yet to be built, and the price he was initially paid for this major project was relatively low, it was nevertheless an important breakthrough for Rodin: he was still a little-known sculptor, and the public commission supplied him with extra confidence, an income and a studio at the government-owned, prestigious Dépôt des Marbres.

Rodin chose *The Divine Comedy*, written by the Italian poet Dante Alighieri (1265–1321) in the early fourteenth century, as the subject of his design for the over-six-metre-high doors. He focused on the first part of the poem, *Inferno*, in which the poet describes a journey through hell. Rodin's ambitious plans involved over 200 figures writhing in torment. These figures became more than illustrations of a story, however. They represented, in the words of Gustave Geffroy (1855–1926), a critic who saw a plaster cast of the doors in 1889, an 'assemblage of action, instinct, destiny, desire, desperation, everything that cries and groans in man.'

Rodin modelled each of the figures separately before incorporating them into the overall structure. This process meant that Rodin was easily able to isolate individual sculptures, so that they could

exist independently of *The Gates of Hell*. Many of Rodin's most celebrated sculptures originated in this way, including *The Thinker*, *The Three Shades* and *The Kiss.*

By 1898 it had become clear that the new decorative arts museum would not require Rodin's doors, as revised plans were made to open it in the Pavillon de Marsan, an existing building which was part of the Louvre. Nevertheless, Rodin continued working on the commission and exhibited *The Gates of Hell,* unfinished and in white plaster, at his successful 1900 exhibition at the Pavillon de l'Alma, Paris. The doors were never completed, and they were only cast in bronze in 1917, shortly after Rodin's death. Despite this, *The Gates of Hell*, rich with figures showing a myriad of human emotions and contorted into every conceivable position, spectacularly demonstrates Rodin's passion. It became more than a project: it was the artist's labour of love, providing inspiration to last a lifetime.

The Gates of Hell, Musée Rodin, Paris, s.1304.

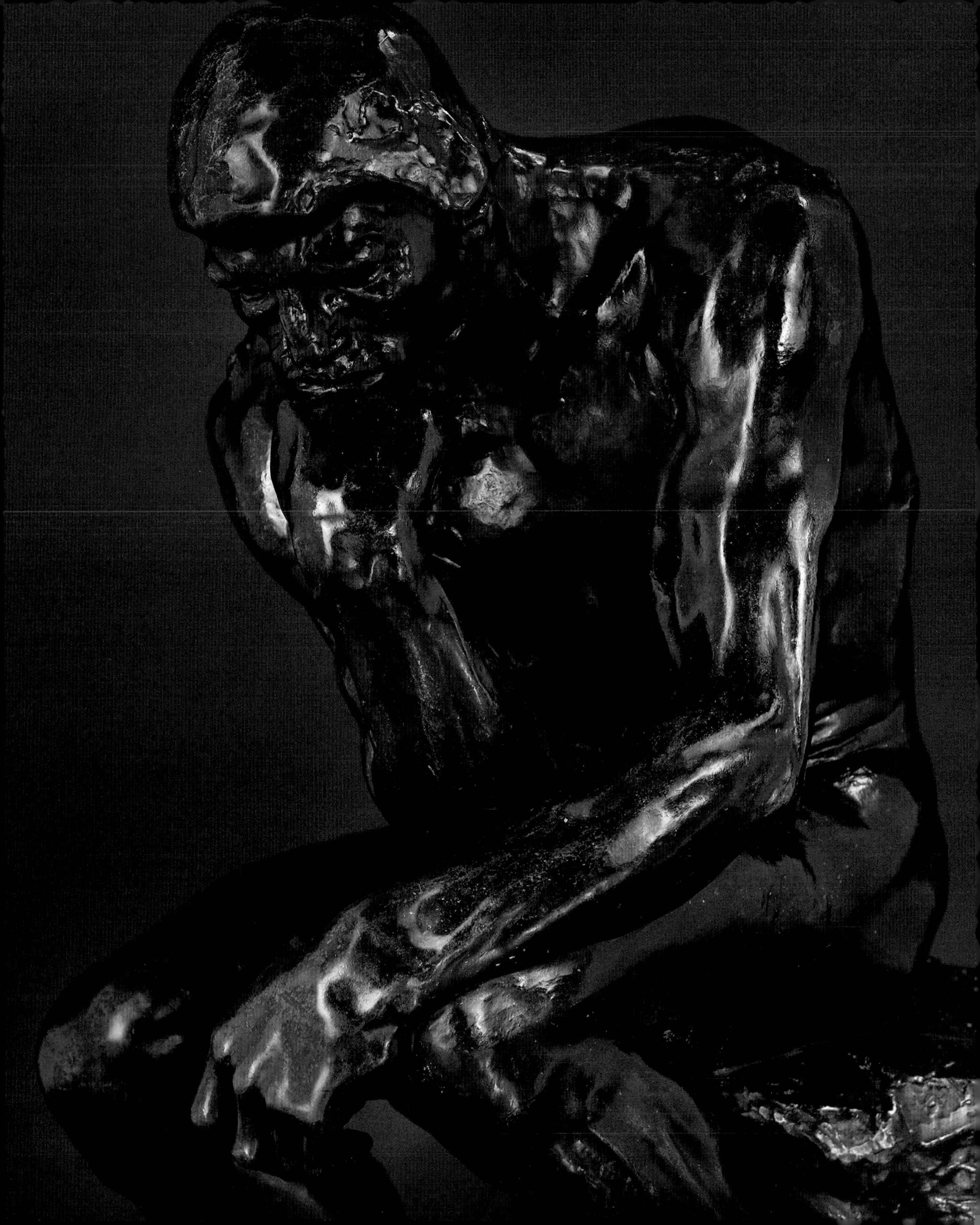

Sculpture in Focus

The Thinker, 1880–81
Cast in bronze by Alexis Rudier Foundry, 1902–22
Bronze
71 x 39 x 58 cm
7.8

Perhaps Rodin's most famous sculpture, *The Thinker*
was one of the first figures made for his 37-year-project
The Gates of Hell, inspired by Dante Alighieri's *Inferno*.
Rodin positioned the figure sitting towards the top of
the portal, looking down. Originally called *The Poet*,
the figure was initially intended to represent Dante and
to be dressed in historical clothing. However, Rodin
soon decided to make the figure nude, giving him a
universality: this could be a man from anywhere, and
from any period in time. Rodin changed the title of the
work, and it soon became known as *The Thinker.*

The body of *The Thinker,* coiled like a spring, suggests
the physical capabilities of man. As Rodin explained,
'What makes my Thinker think is that he thinks not only
with his brain, with his knitted brow, his distended nostrils
and compressed lips, but with every muscle of his arms,
back, and legs, with his clenched fist and gripping toes.'
The figure's distinctive pose is similar to a sculpture of
Lorenzo de Medici (1449–92) by the Italian Renaissance
artist Michelangelo Buonarroti (1475–1564), who Rodin
admired, as well as the tormented *Ugolino and his Sons*,
also inspired by *Inferno*, by Jean-Baptiste Carpeaux
(1827–75), part of the generation of French sculptors
working just before Rodin.

Originally modelled in clay and then cast in plaster around
1880, the first bronze cast of *The Thinker* was made
around 1884 and exhibited in 1888. It was subsequently
enlarged, with one such version used for the sculptor's
grave in Meudon, France. From 1902 onwards, the
Alexis Rudier Foundry, Paris – established by Rodin's
trusted founder Alexis Rudier (d. 1897) – produced
about 30 casts of the original size, including the
sculpture which was bought by William Burrell
in 1922.

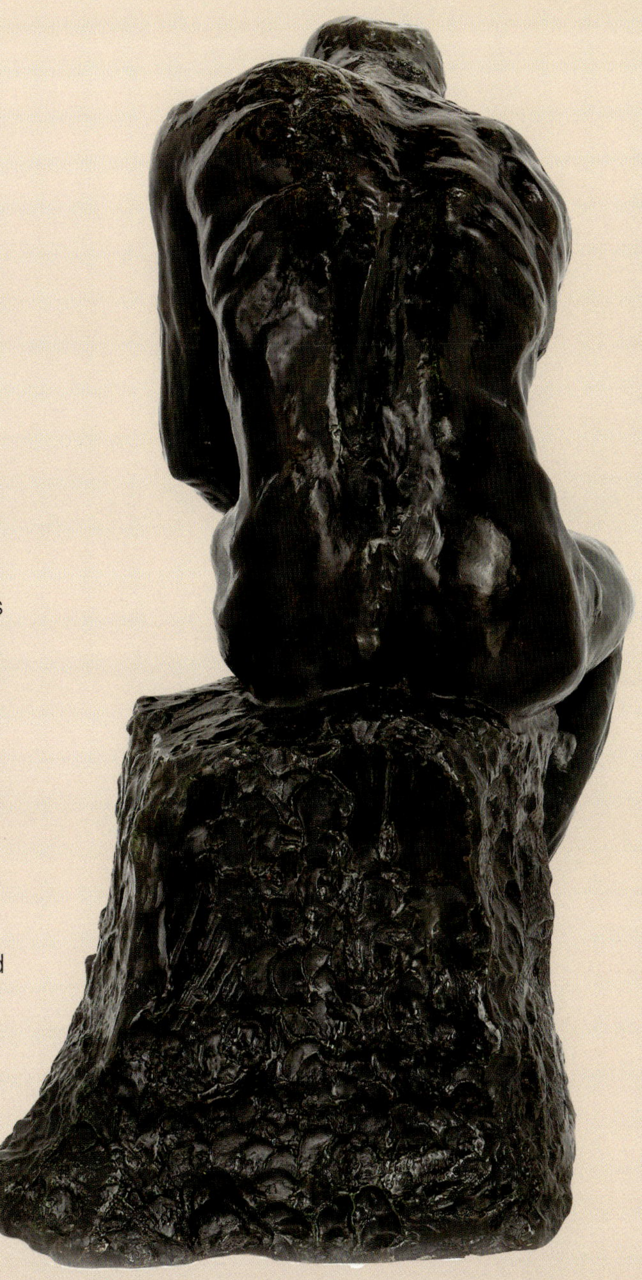

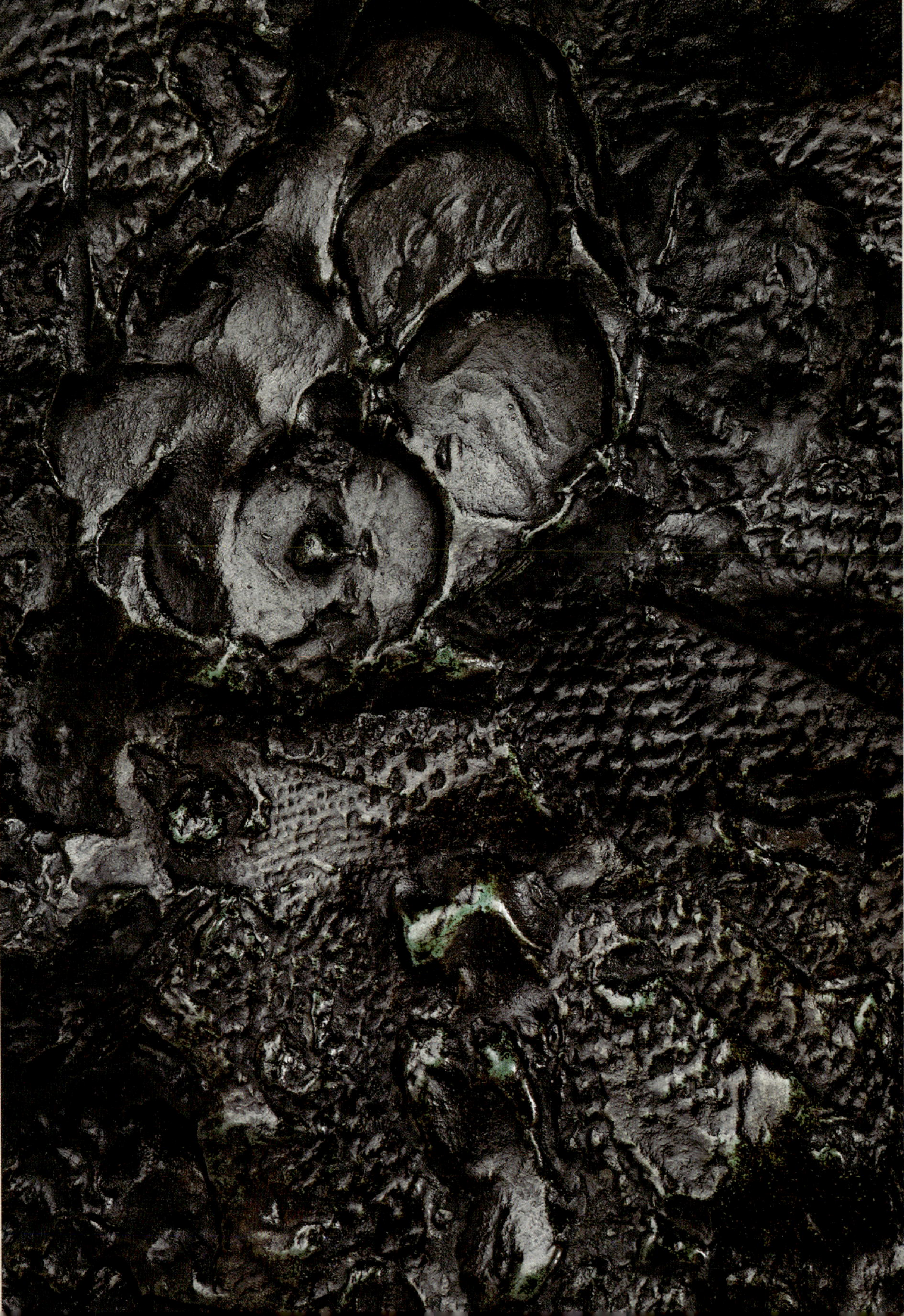

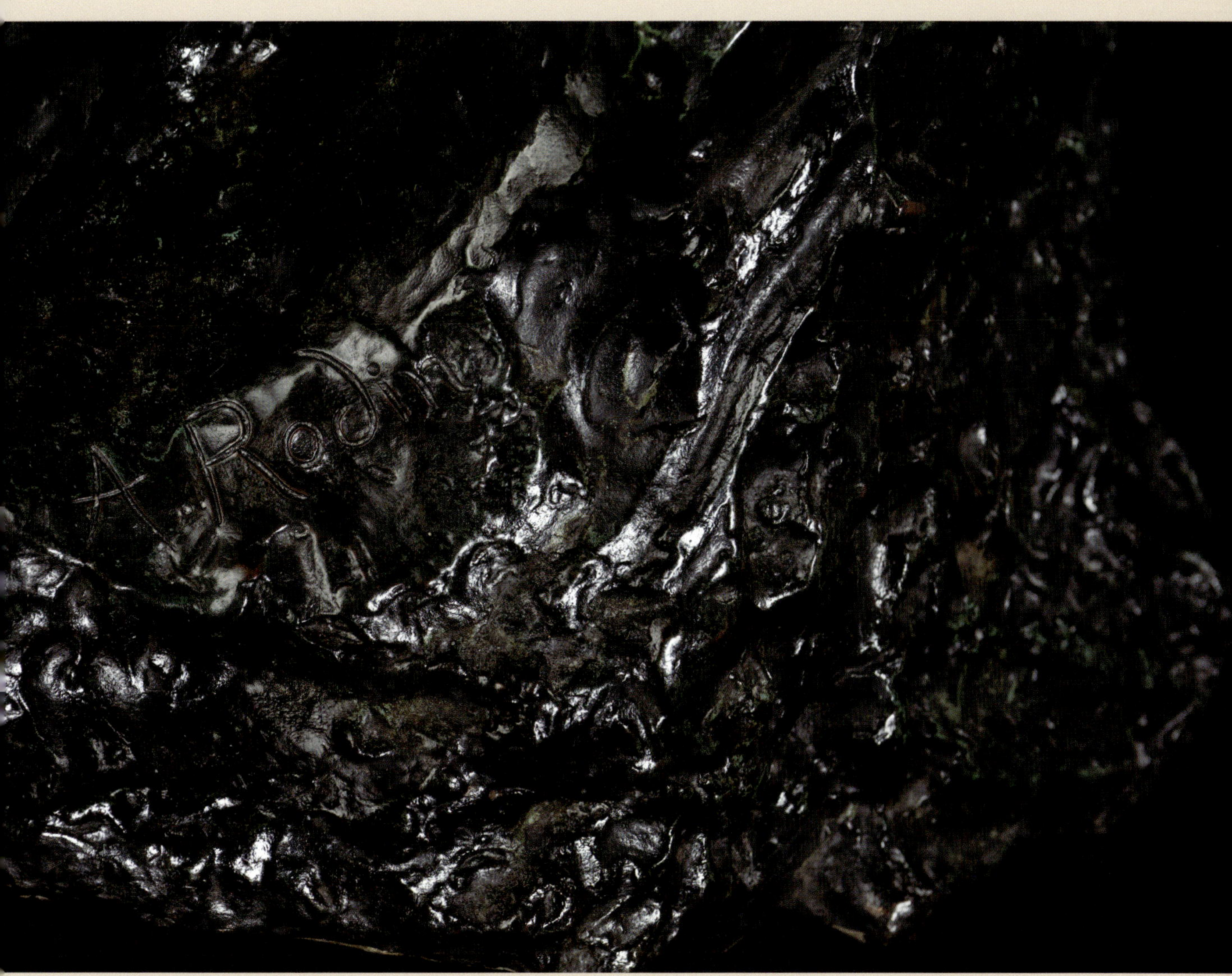

Before the clay sculpture of *The Thinker* was cast in plaster and then bronze, Rodin left marks in the still soft clay. Imprints resembling fingernails can be seen in the base of the sculpture (left) and marks made by his fingers appear near his signature (above).

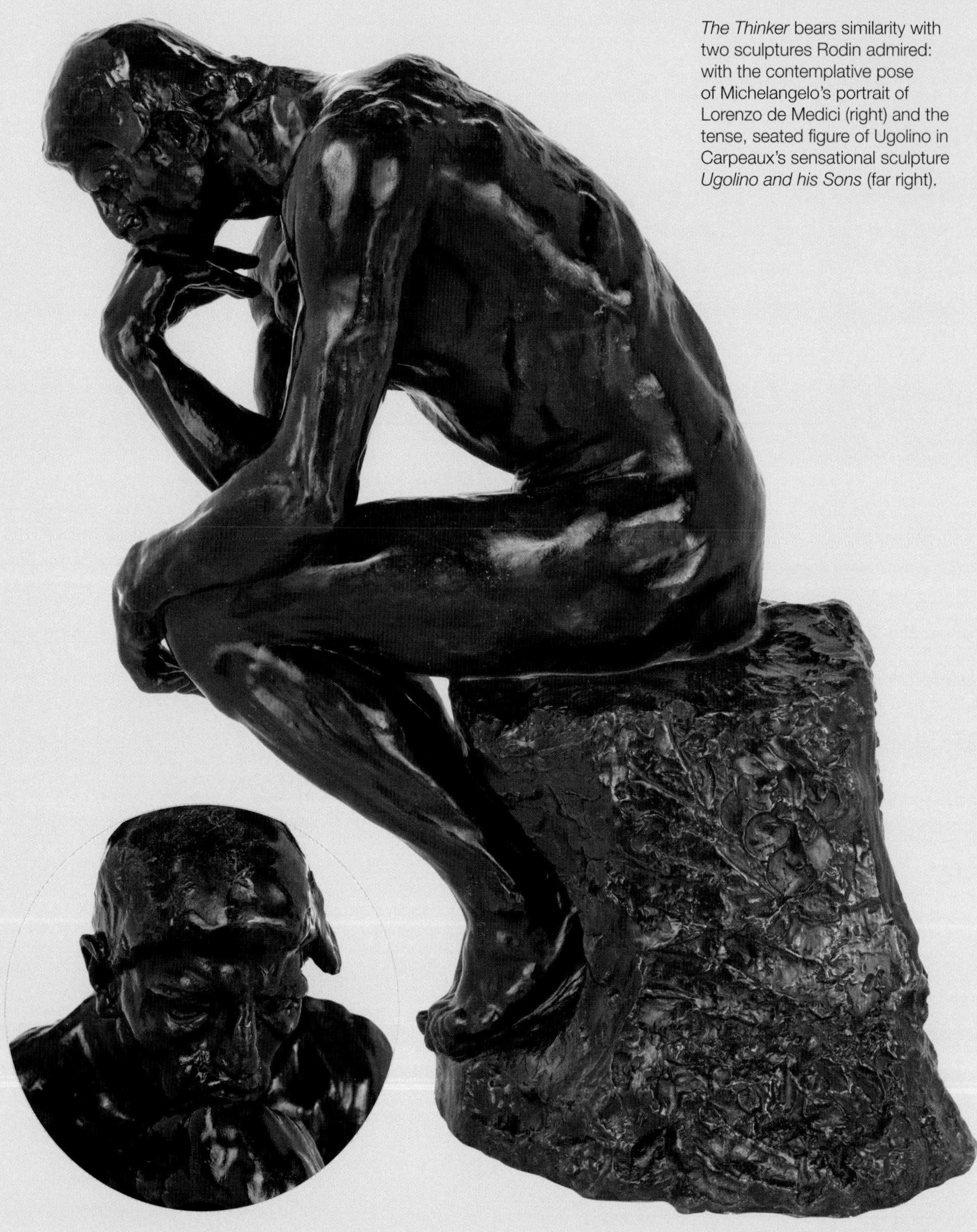

The Thinker bears similarity with two sculptures Rodin admired: with the contemplative pose of Michelangelo's portrait of Lorenzo de Medici (right) and the tense, seated figure of Ugolino in Carpeaux's sensational sculpture *Ugolino and his Sons* (far right).

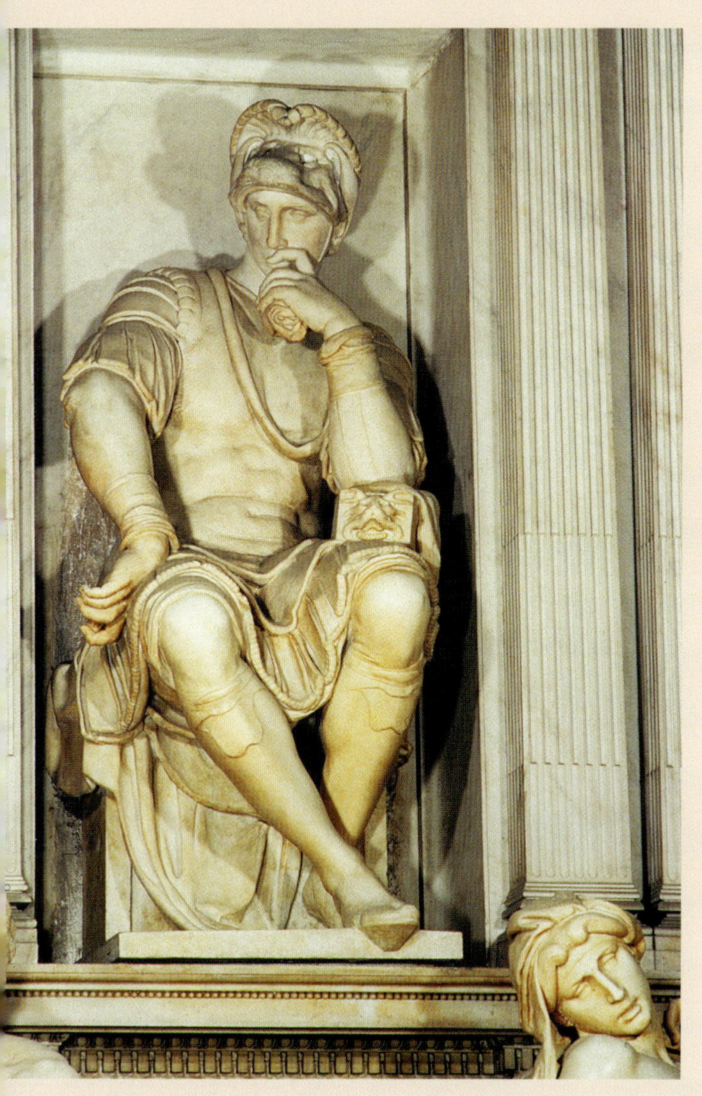

Lorenzo de Medici, 1521–24, by Michelangelo, marble. Tomb of the Medicis, Florence.

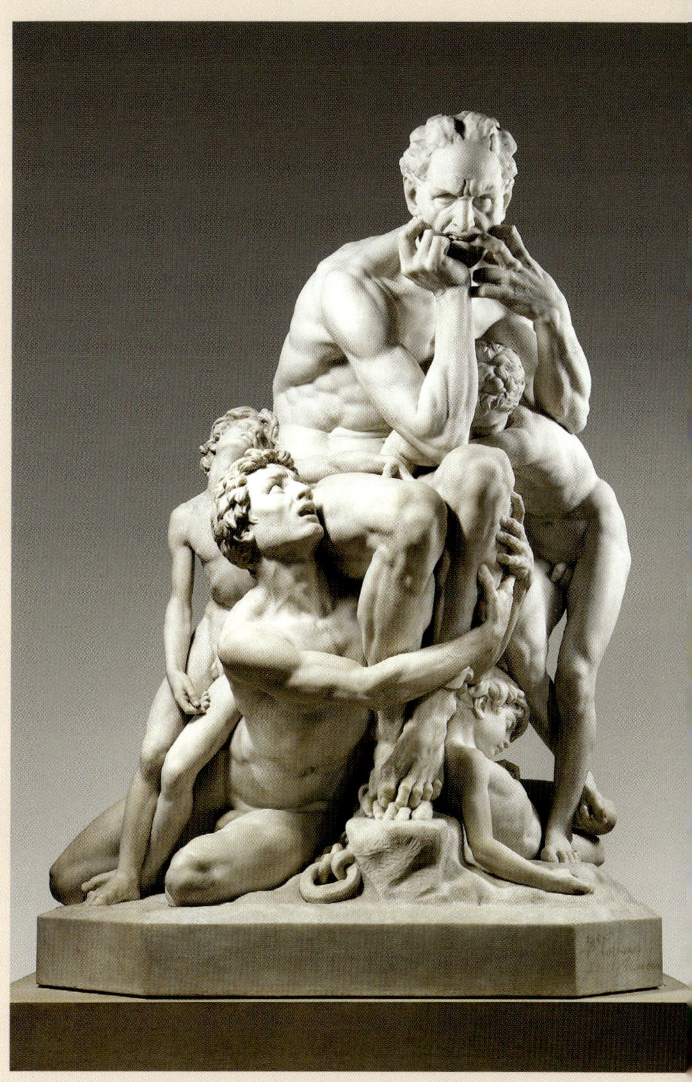

Ugolino and His Sons, 1865–67, by Jean-Baptiste Carpeaux, marble. Metropolitan Museum of Art, New York, 67.250.

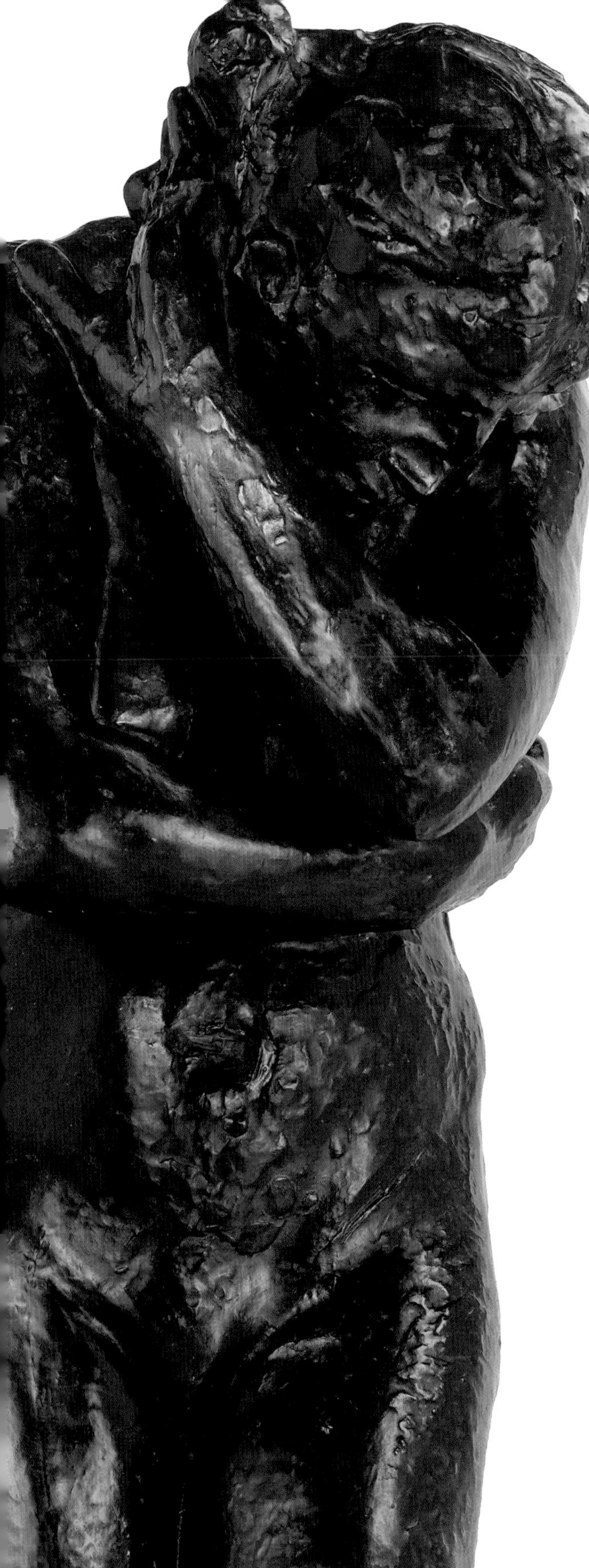

Eve After the Fall, 1880–81
Cast in bronze by Alexis Rudier Foundry, 1928
Bronze
170 x 49 x 60 cm
7.19

Like many of his most famous sculptures, *Eve After the Fall* was first intended to feature as part of *The Gates of Hell*. *Eve* would flank the gates, along with *Adam*, a sculpture of her biblical counterpart. Both figures, however, were omitted from the design, and were instead shown as individual sculptures.

While *Adam* was finished by 1881, the journey of *Eve* was less straightforward. After sculpting this work over several sessions, Rodin noticed that the body of his model for Eve – likely one of his favourite models, Adèle or Maria Abbruzzesi – was changing. Having to regularly rework the sculpture's pelvis, Rodin soon discovered that the model was pregnant. Before long, posing in the cold studio became too uncomfortable for her to continue, forcing Rodin to prematurely finish work on the sculpture. He later described the model being pregnant as a 'fortunate accident', which helped to give *Eve* character.

Despite being first modelled in 1881, *Eve After the Fall* was not cast in bronze until 1897 and Rodin was not ready to show the sculpture until 1899. It had been left unfinished when the model for *Eve* stopped posing, with a rough and uneven surface. Obvious fingerprints and other marks were left on the surface, allowing us a tantalizing glimpse into the way that Rodin worked the clay. Even the metal armature – the metal structure which provided a supporting framework for the clay – is still visible on her right ankle. By the time Rodin returned to this sculpture nearly two decades after he started it, his style had changed to a point where he was willing to embrace and exhibit what he would originally have seen as imperfect.

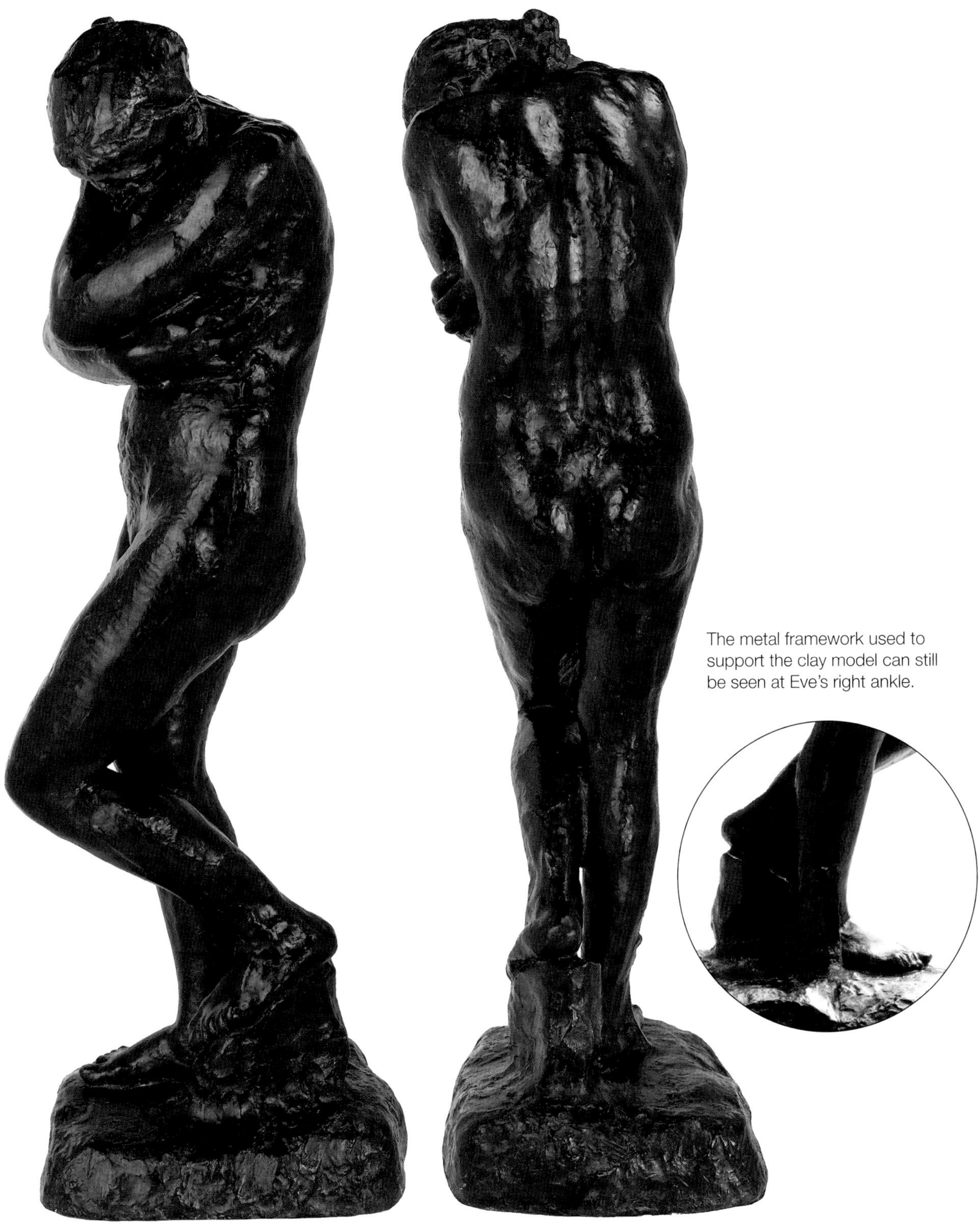

The metal framework used to support the clay model can still be seen at Eve's right ankle.

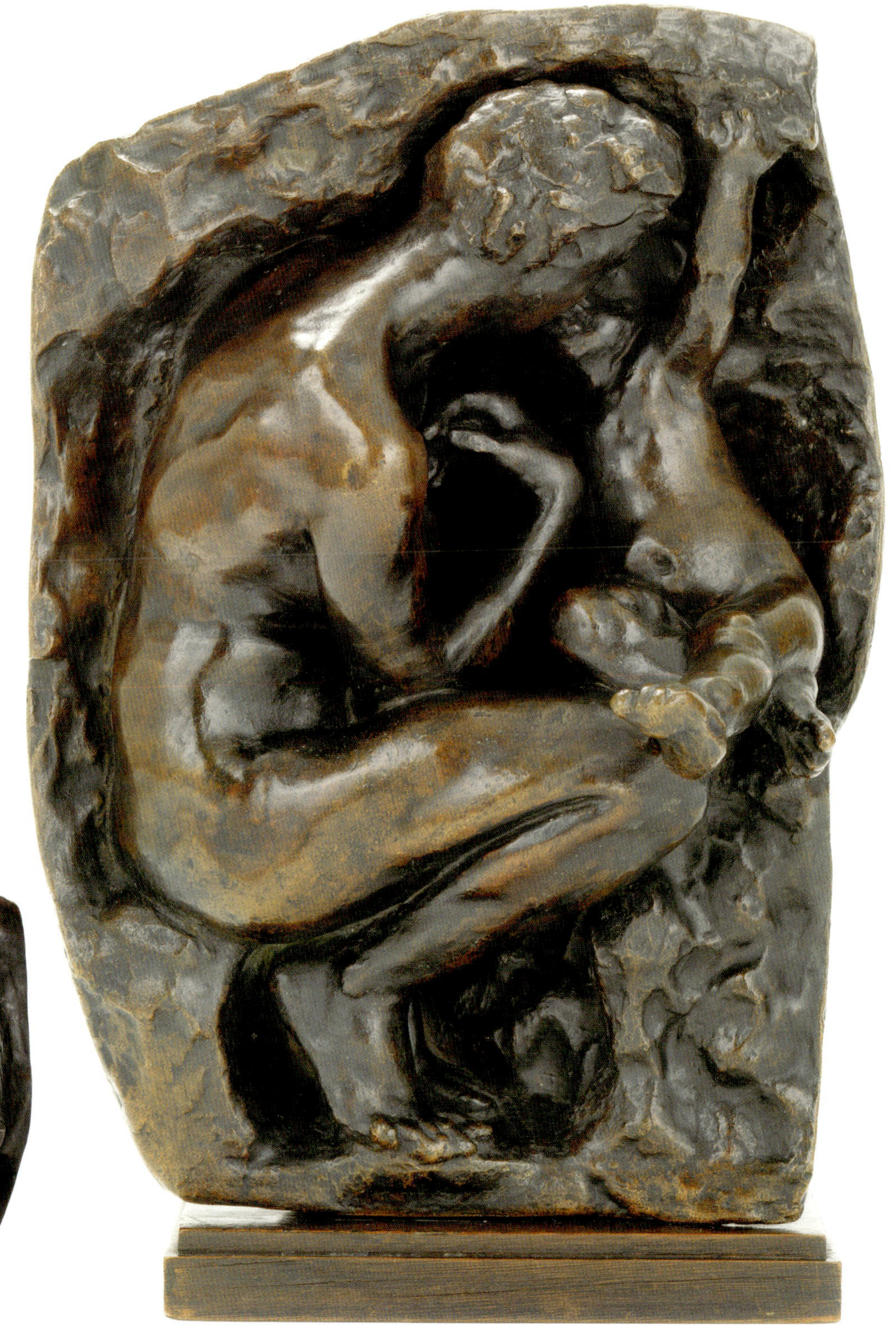

Below: The back of the sculpture shows part of the metal rods used to create a strong core during the casting process.

Mother and Child in the Grotto, about 1885
Cast in bronze before 1911
Bronze
40 x 26.5 x 22 cm
7.17

Sometimes we are able to see the way Rodin
manipulated the clay he modelled by the marks
on the surface of a sculpture. In this work, Rodin's
trademark pinches and pulls of clay – which can still
be seen in the bronze cast – helped to create the
appearance of a protective, rocky surround, in which
a mother sits and gently kisses her small child.

Rodin first started to depict images of women with
infants when he was living and working in Belgium,
between 1871 and 1877. These were heavily
influenced by the sculptor Albert-Ernest Carrier-
Belleuse (1824–87), for whom Rodin worked at the
time, and whose designs were decorative, pretty
and reminiscent of the eighteenth-century Rococo
style. The theme interested Rodin again in the
1890s, when he produced several small groups
showing maternal or fraternal love, including this
one. These later sculptures were simpler, and more
typical of his signature style.

Originally, Rodin intended *Mother and Child in the
Grotto* to be part of *The Gates of Hell.* Perhaps
Rodin concluded that the gentle subject of this work
did not fit within the dramatic theme of the larger
work, because by 1888 he had omitted it from the
scheme. Rodin found other uses for the sculpture:
in 1886 *Mother and Child in the Grotto* was included
as part of a design to decorate a building for his
French patron, Maurice Fenaille (1855–1937). It was
also cast 28 times in bronze for collectors, including
an early cast that Rodin gave to the painter Claude
Monet (1840–1926) as a token of friendship, as well
as this example.

This sculpture is known by several different names,
including *Maternal Tenderness*, *Shell Woman and
Child* and *Young Mother.* It may have been the
sculpture William Burrell lent to the 1901 Glasgow
International Exhibition, which was listed in the
exhibition catalogue as *Maternal Love.* However,

we cannot be certain: the 1901 loan could equally
have been *Fleeting Love* (pp. 48–51) or *Brother and
Sister* (pp. 38–39), or even, theoretically, another
sculpture which Burrell bought and sold without
recording.

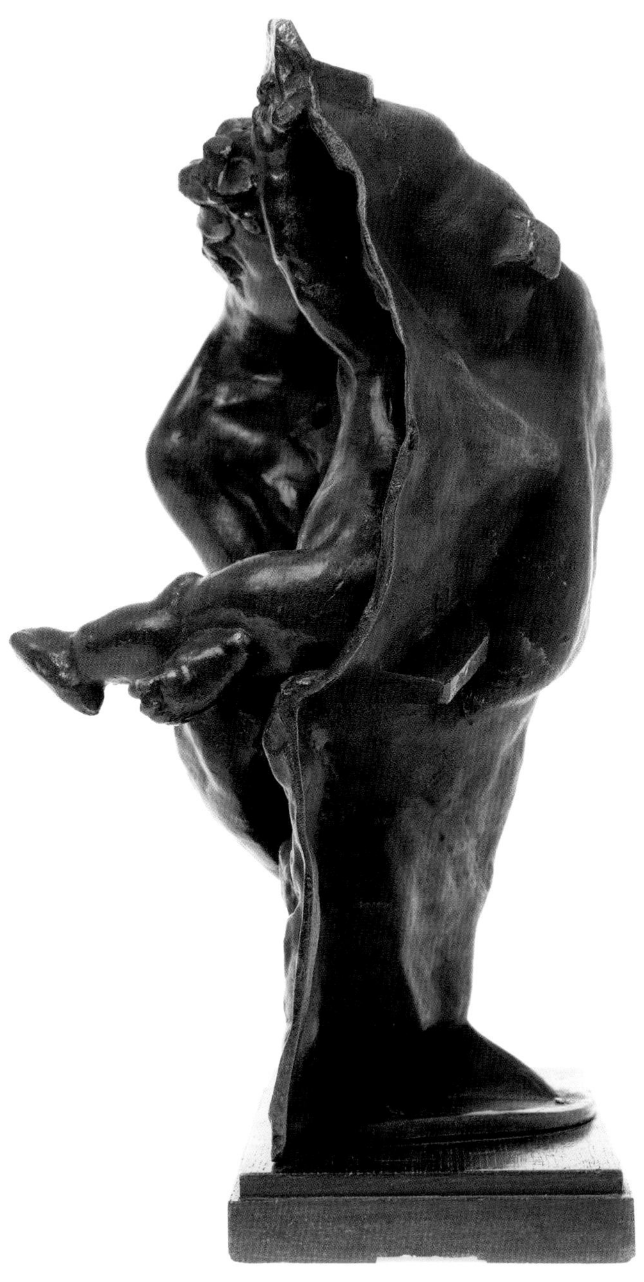

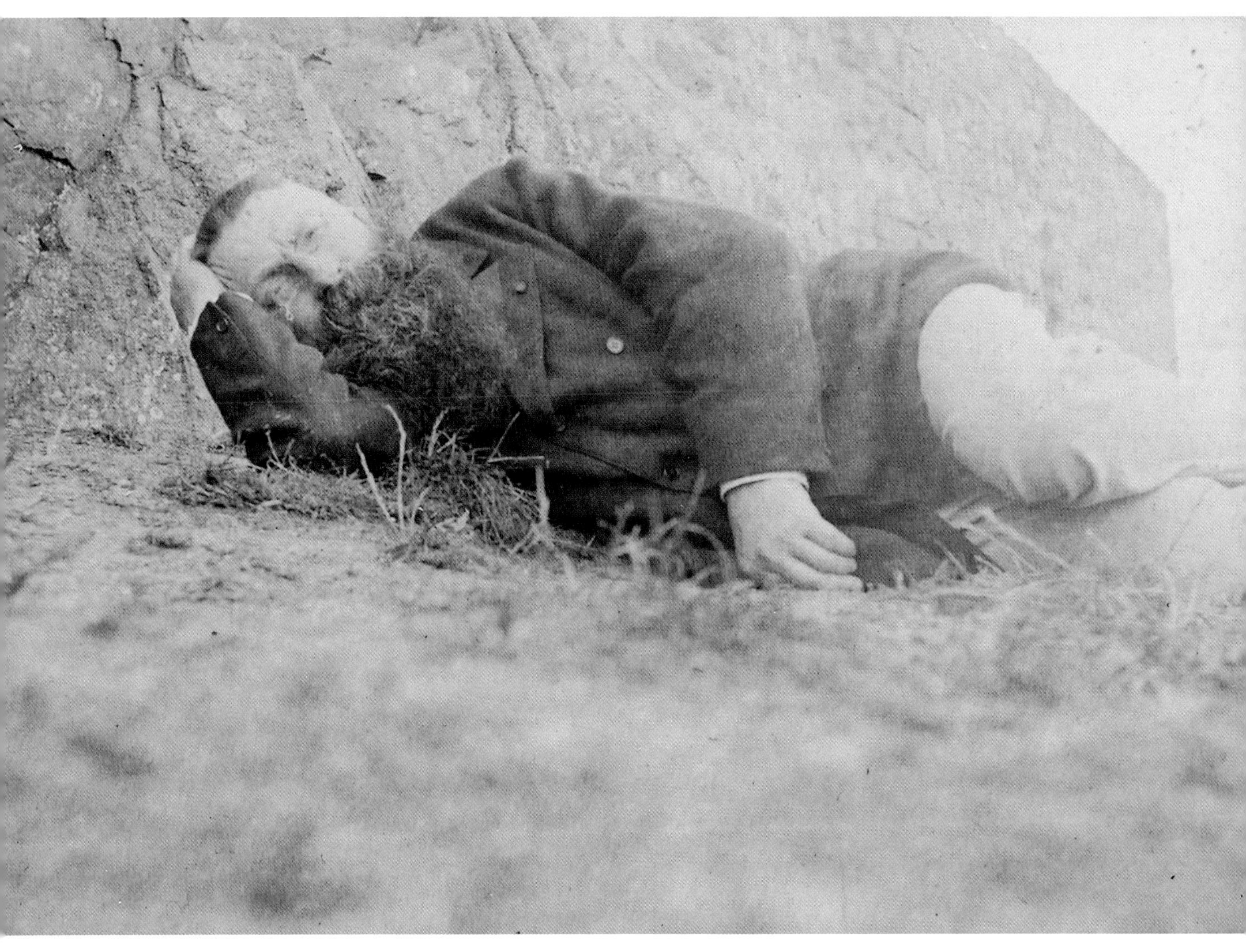

Above: One of Rodin's most important principles was an obedience to nature. He once said, 'I do not correct nature, I incorporate myself into it; it directs me.' Auguste Rodin, about 1893, Guernsey. Musée Rodin, Paris, Ph.172.

Opposite: In 1882 Camille Claudel rented a studio where she worked alongside other women sculptors. Shown on the left, Claudel is sculpting one of her first major works, *Sakountala*. Her friend Jessie Lipscomb (1861–1952) can be seen on the right. Camille Claudel and Jessie Lipscomb in the atelier at No. 117 Rue Notre-Dame-des-Champs, 1887, by William Elborne. Musée Rodin, Paris, Ph.1773.

Rodin's Inspiration

Beauty, Rodin believed, lay in nature. He rejected the lack of realism in most French sculpture of his time, and instead sought truth through close observation. After using a life model for the first time in 1863, for his earliest major sculpture *The Man with a Broken Nose*, Rodin always worked with models. He selected people of all ages, shapes and sizes, such as the older woman who modelled for his memorable *She Who Was the Helmet Maker's Once-Beautiful Wife*.

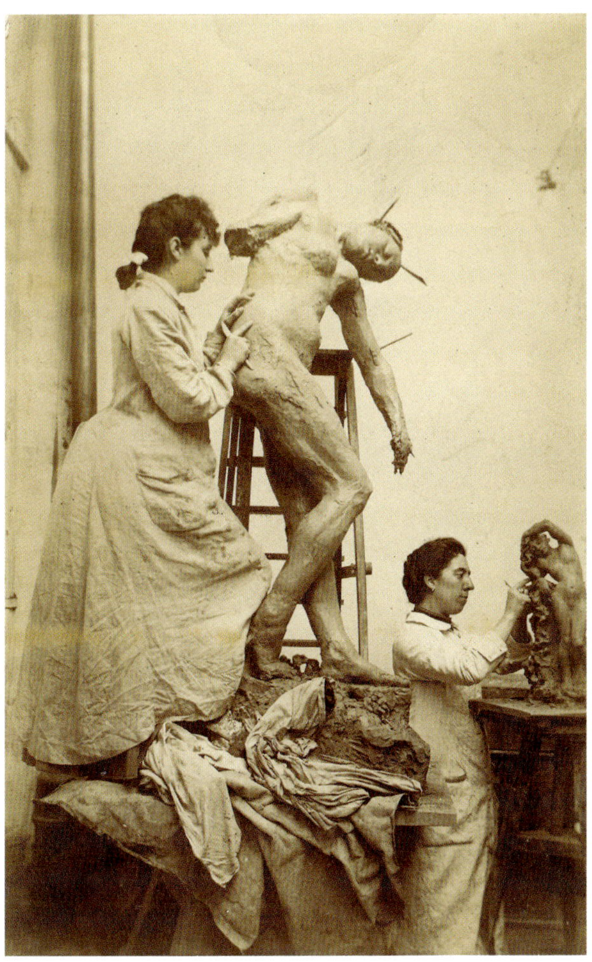

One of the most important influences on Rodin was the work of Michelangelo, whom Rodin later declared to be 'my master and my idol'. Rodin made his first visit to Italy in 1876, determined to see first-hand the beauty of the great sculptor's work. He wrote to his lifelong partner Rose Beuret, 'since the moment I got to Florence I've been studying Michelangelo – that won't surprise you, and I think the great magician is going to give me some of his secrets.' Instead of the conventional, formulaic qualities of contemporary sculpture, which showed classical and graceful poses, Michelangelo's figures were powerful, forceful and showed the body twisted at dramatic angles. In Italy, Rodin roamed around, notebook in hand, drawing the curves and contortions of the hips, necks and elbows seen in Michelangelo's sculpture. The young sculptor's eyes were opened by the Italian's way of breathing life into the body, truly animating it with strong and dynamic poses. Michelangelo's influence on Rodin can be detected in many of his finest sculptures, particularly the distinctive pose of the figure in *The Age of Bronze*, which is reminiscent of Michelangelo's *The Dying Slave* (pp. 14–17).

Between the years 1883 and 1893, Rodin's all-consuming affair with Camille Claudel (1864–1943) provided plentiful inspiration for the artist. Claudel was a young sculptor working in Paris, at a time when women still were not accepted as students into the city's prestigious art school, the École des Beaux-Arts. Her skill was spotted by Rodin when she was just 17 years old, and he was 42. Soon after meeting, the pair became romantically involved. Two years later, Claudel came to work in Rodin's studio and was trusted with challenging tasks including modelling the hands and feet of figures. Inspired by his young and beautiful lover, Rodin created a number of sculptures that focus on passionate love, including one of his most famous artworks, *The Kiss*.

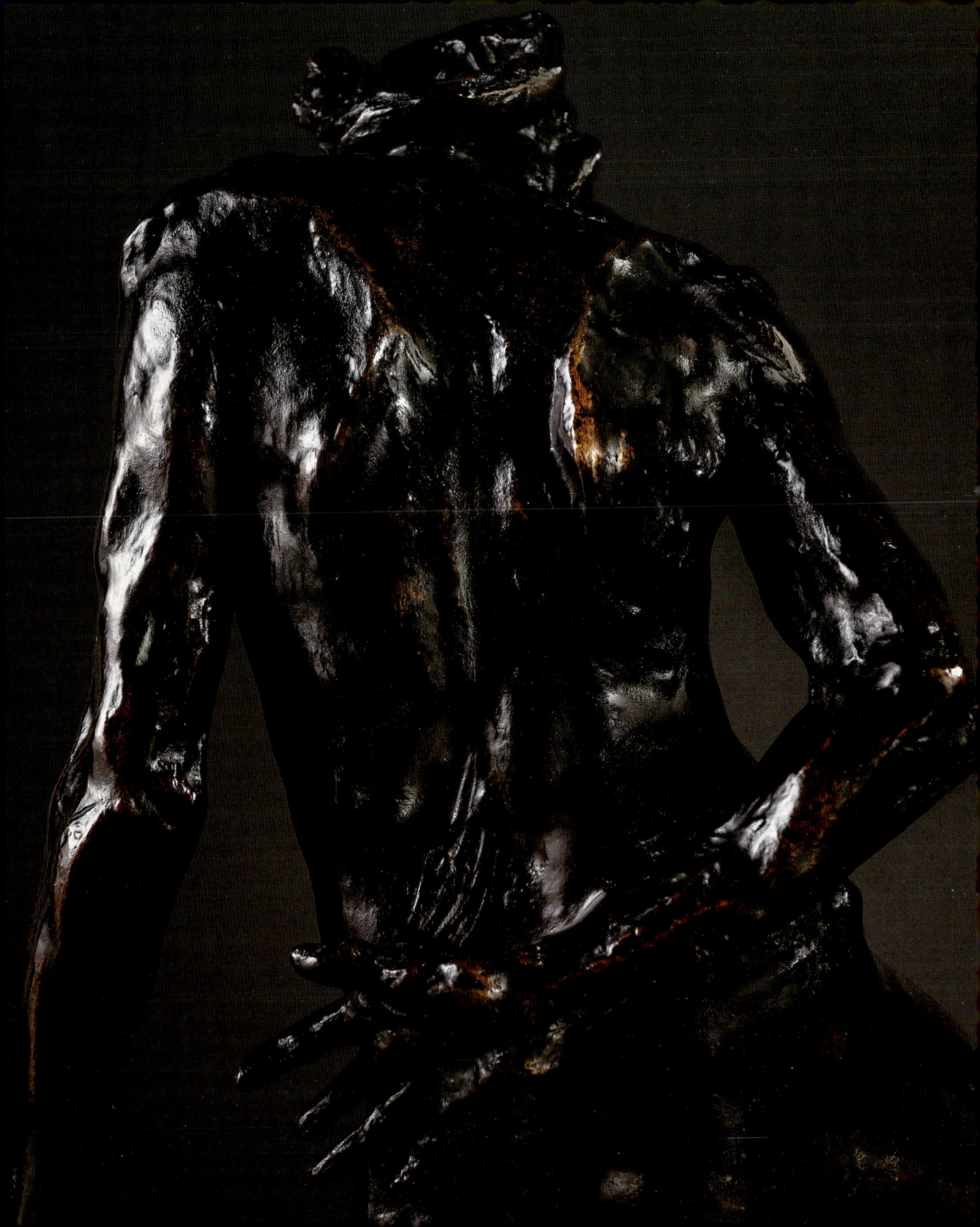

Sculpture in Focus

She Who Was the Helmet Maker's
Once-Beautiful Wife, 1885–87
Cast in bronze before 1889
Bronze
50.5 x 32 x 23.5 cm
7.7

Rodin was fascinated by human bodies, and not just those of attractive young models, as were popular in mainstream sculpture. He believed, 'in art, only what has *character* is beautiful. *Character* is the intense truth of any natural spectacle, whether beautiful or ugly … And what is regarded as ugly in Nature often shows more character than what is described as beautiful … For the artist worthy of this name, everything is beautiful in Nature.'

Rodin based *She Who Was the Helmet Maker's Once-Beautiful Wife*, his vivid depiction of the effects of aging, on an elderly Italian woman called Maria Caira, who also modelled for the sculpture *Misery* by Rodin's friend and collaborator Jules Desbois (1851–1935), and *Clotho* by Camille Claudel.

The sculpture was first exhibited as *Old Woman*, revealing Rodin's original intention to simply depict the human body at an advanced age. In 1891 a cast was purchased by the French state, and the current title was first used. Rodin often created his sculptures first, before finding titles that matched them later on. Linking the sculptures to poems or stories appealed to his literary interests. It also sometimes made them more understandable to a public who were not used to seeing studies of human bodies presented without such references. The name the sculpture was given refers to a poem by the fifteenth-century French writer François Villon (1431–63), in which a woman sadly laments the effects of old age.

When I think back on the good times,
what I once was, what I've become,
or when I see my body naked,
and see myself completely changed,
dried up, paltry, thin and scrawny,
I'm nearly driven mad with rage.

What has become of that smooth brow,
that blond hair, those arching eyebrows,
and well-spaced eyes, that playful look
that snared the most refined of men;
the fine, straight nose, not large or small,
those small and well-positioned ears,
dimpled chin and clear, bright skin,
and lovely vermilion lips?

From *The Testament* by François Villon, 1461

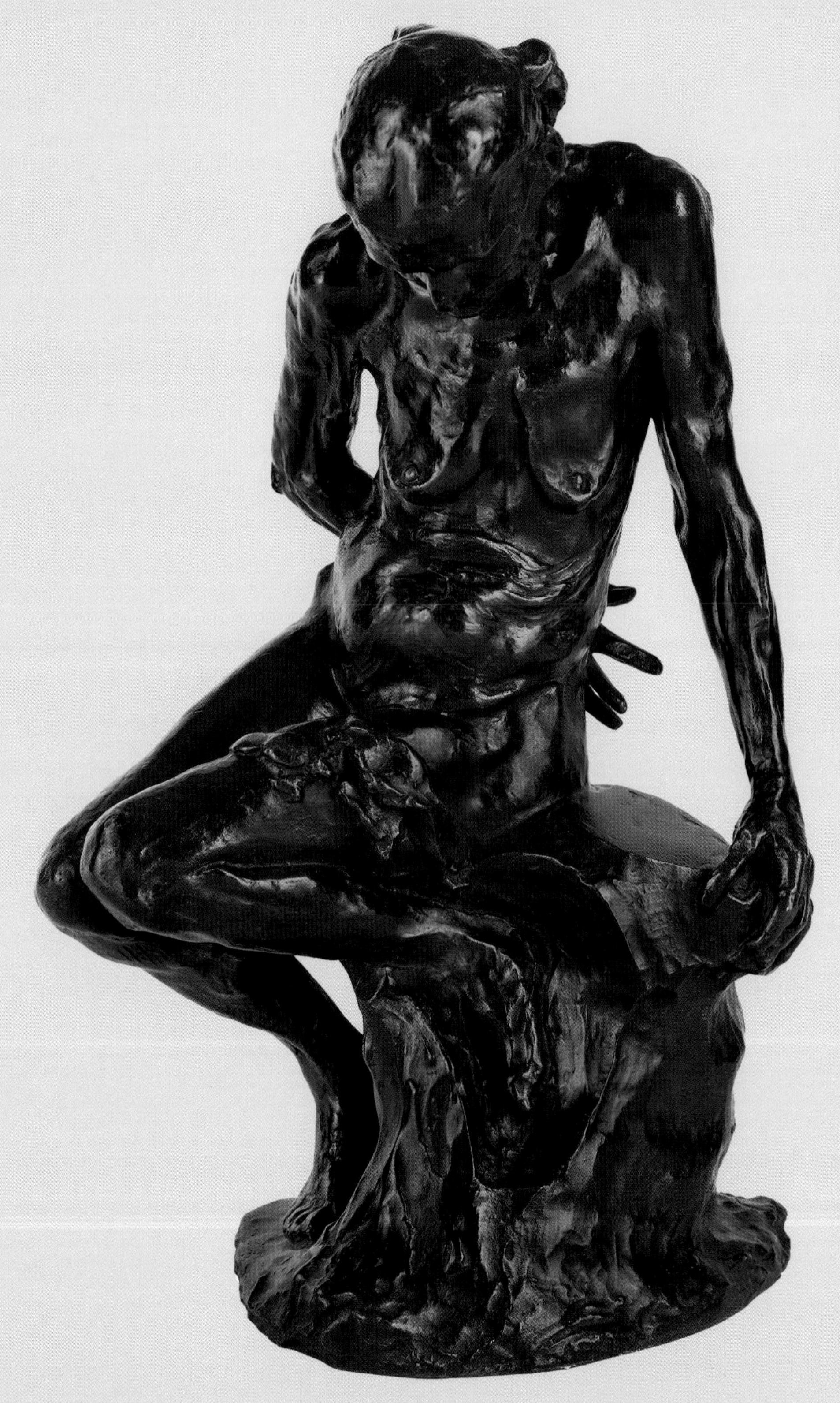

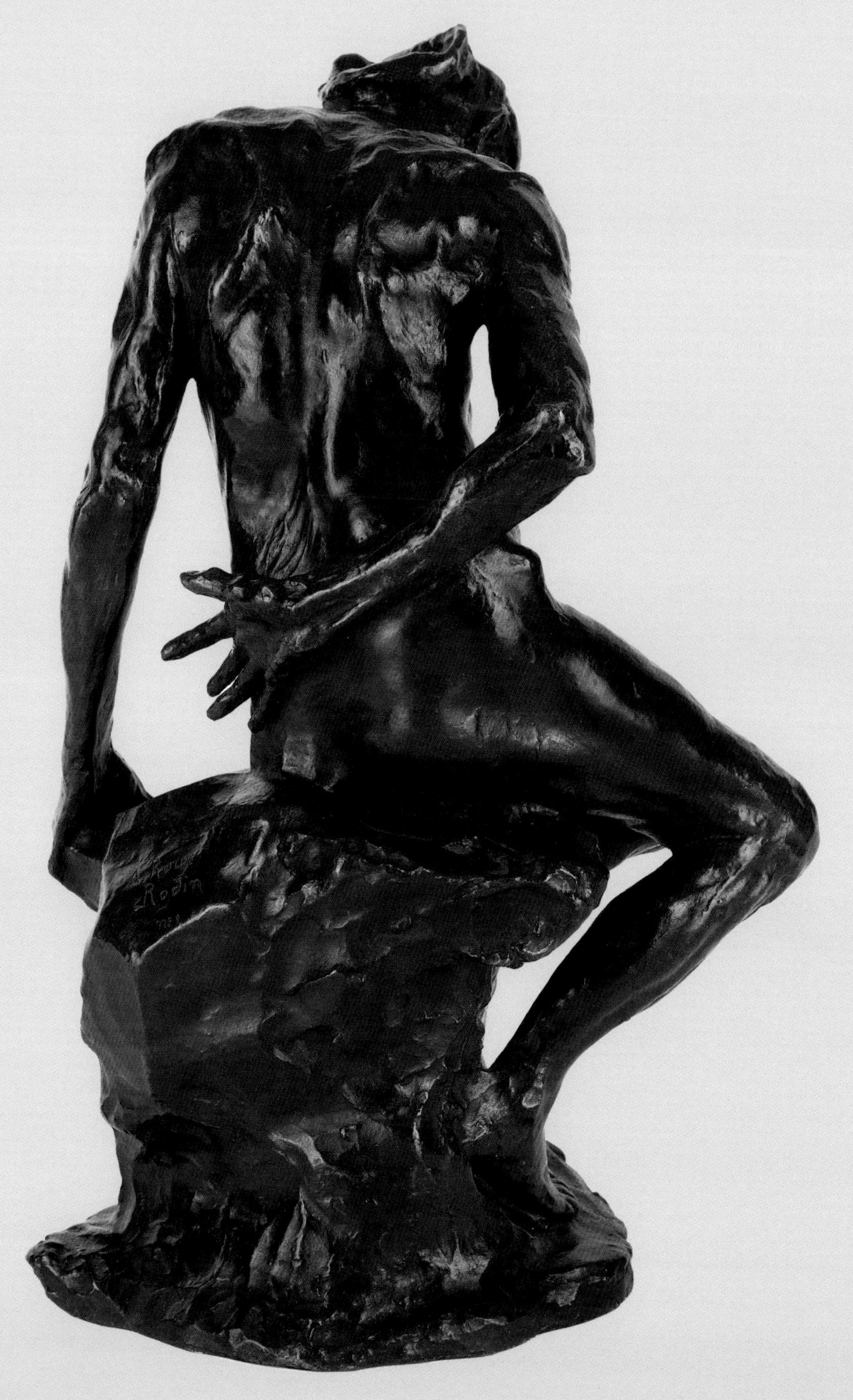

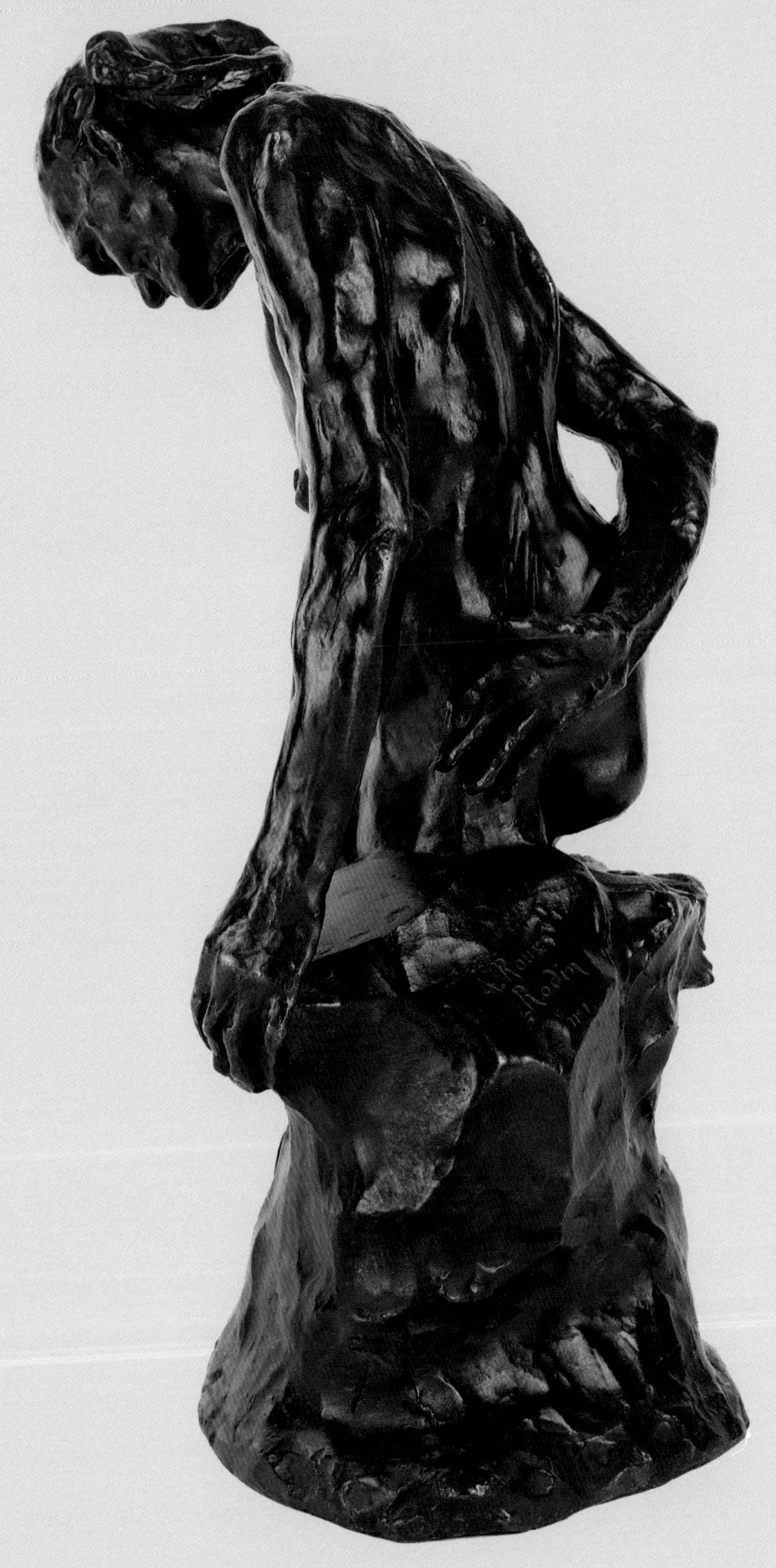

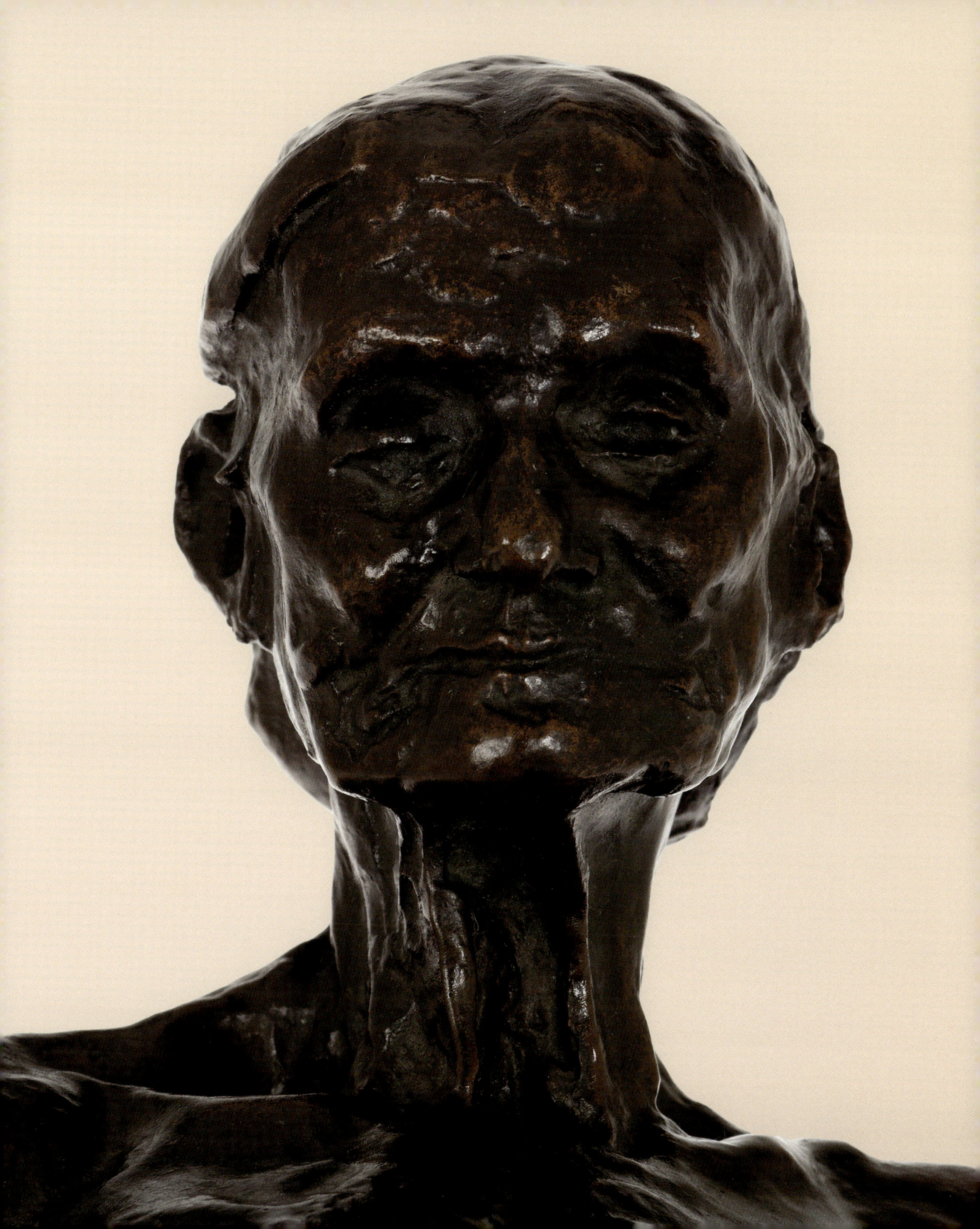

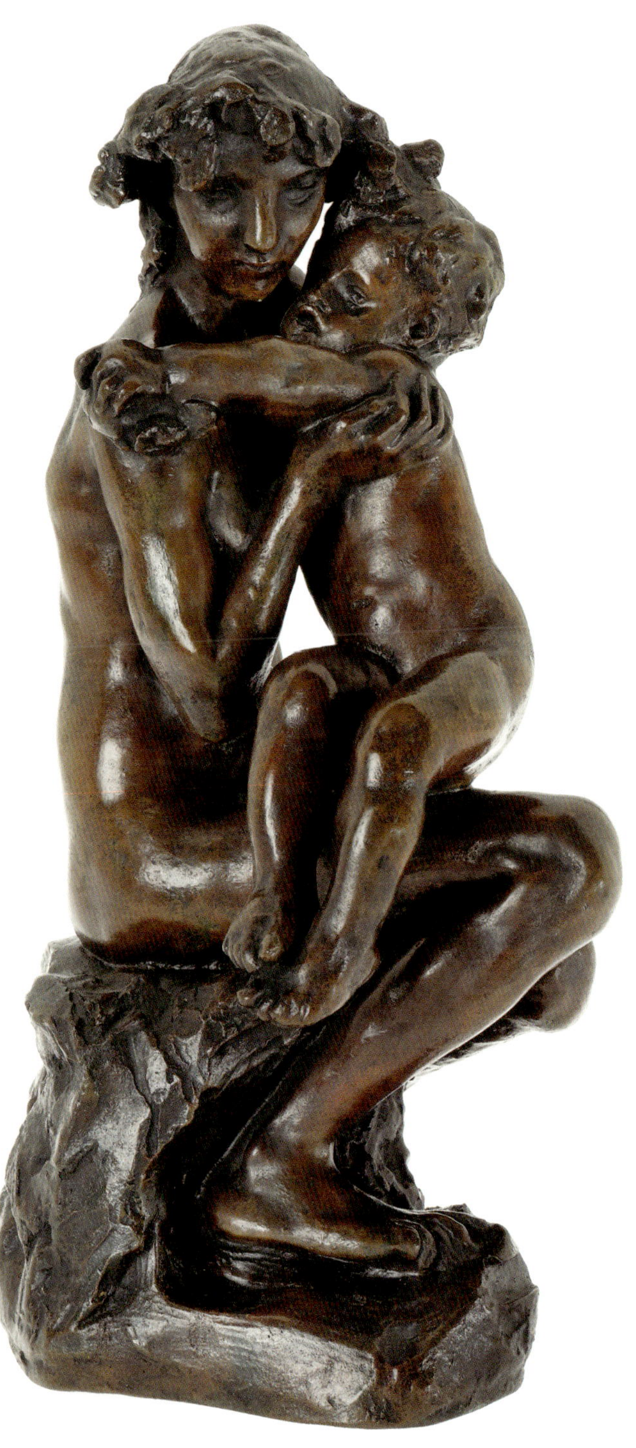

Brother and Sister, 1890–91
Cast in bronze before 1911
Bronze
38.3 x 18 x 20 cm
7.13

Although Rodin spent decades with his partner Rose Beuret, whom he eventually married in 1917, the artist is known to have had affairs with other women, including models and sitters. His tempestuous relationship with the sculptor Camille Claudel is the most famous. It had such an impact on the artist that their passion directly influenced his artwork.

Claudel started working in Rodin's studio in 1884, and by then they were involved in a relationship that Rodin described as 'atrocious madness', the artist begging to see Claudel every day. During the mid 1880s, Rodin's art often featured tormented and passionate love as its subject, for example *I am Beautiful* and *Eternal Springtime*. These were the early years of Claudel and Rodin's relationship, a time of passion that clearly spilled over into Rodin's artwork. During those years, the pair were often together, writing letters and arranging trysts both at home and while abroad. Their lives and work became so inextricably linked that it can be hard to tell their sculptures apart. It is only recently that several of Claudel's designs have been disentangled from Rodin's.

Brother and Sister is the only example where the designs of both artists are clearly unified in one sculpture. The female figure in this sculpture derives from an artwork by Camille Claudel, *Young Girl with a Sheaf of Wheat* (right), which was made in 1886–87. Rodin made *Brother and Sister* several years later, after another small sculpture, *Galatea* (far right), which follows a similar pose to Claudel's *Young Girl with a Sheaf of Wheat*. *Brother and Sister* moves closer still to Claudel's sculpture, to the point where it looks almost identical, particularly noticeable in the girl's angular face. For his work, Rodin altered Claudel's design by removing the sheaf of wheat at the girl's back and placing an infant on her knees.

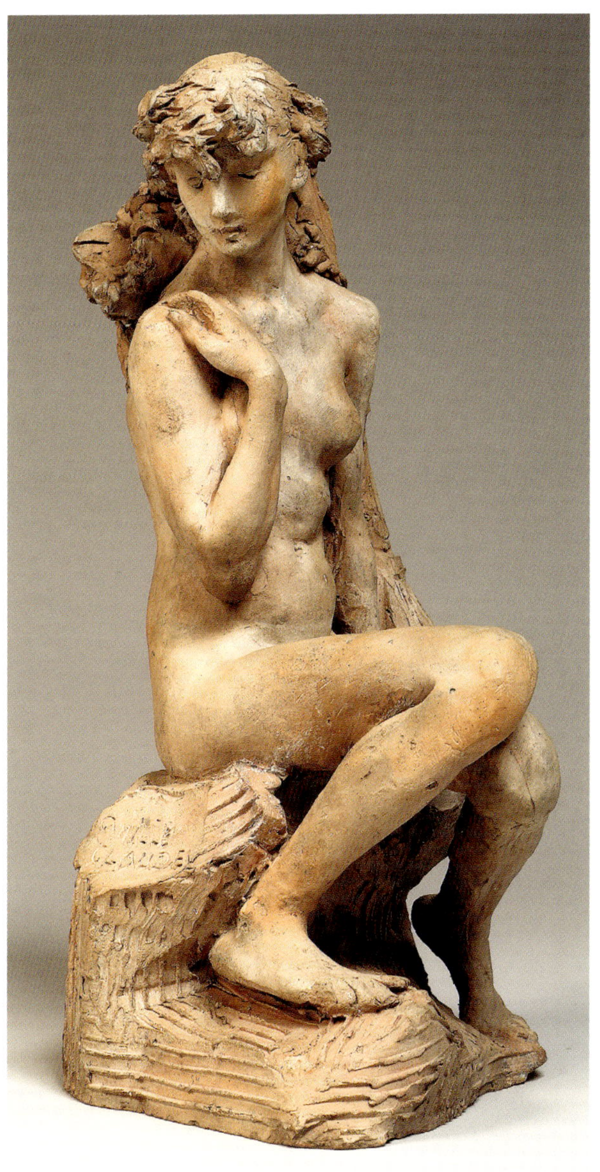

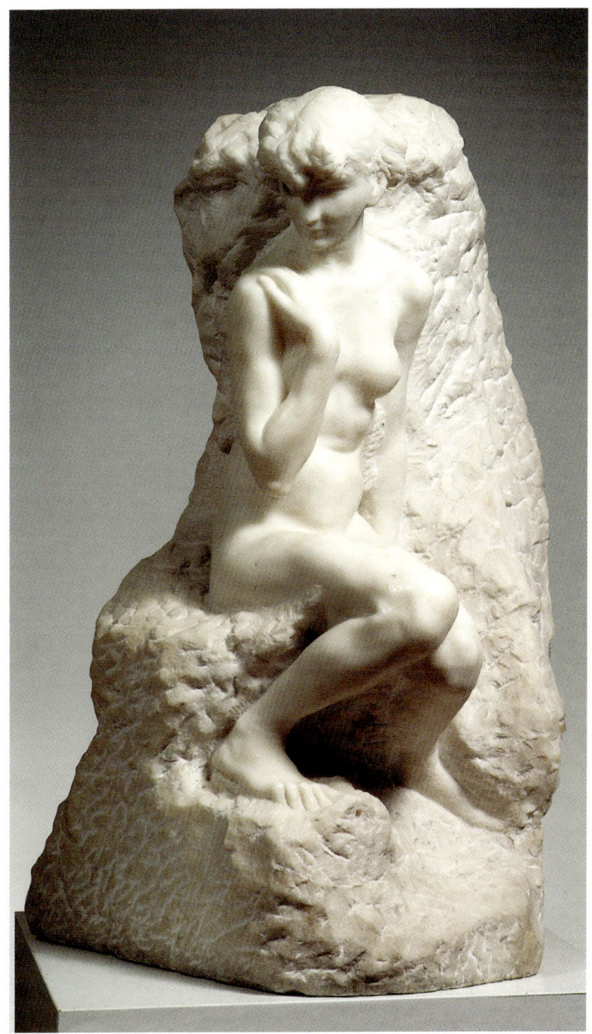

Above left and above: Camille Claudel sculpted *Young Girl with a Sheaf of Wheat* (above left) about three years before Rodin created his own versions: first, his marble *Galatea* (above), and then *Brother and Sister* (opposite). *Young Girl with a Sheaf of Wheat*, 1886–87, by Camille Claudel, terracotta, Musée Rodin, Paris, s.6738. *Galatea*, about 1887, by Auguste Rodin, marble. Musée Rodin, Paris, s.1110.

Claudel is often cited as taking inspiration from Rodin, and was even criticized in her lifetime for copying the work of Rodin; however, the influence clearly worked both ways. *Brother and Sister* is a charming and rare example of the closeness between the artists, and the inspiration that Rodin found in Claudel's art.

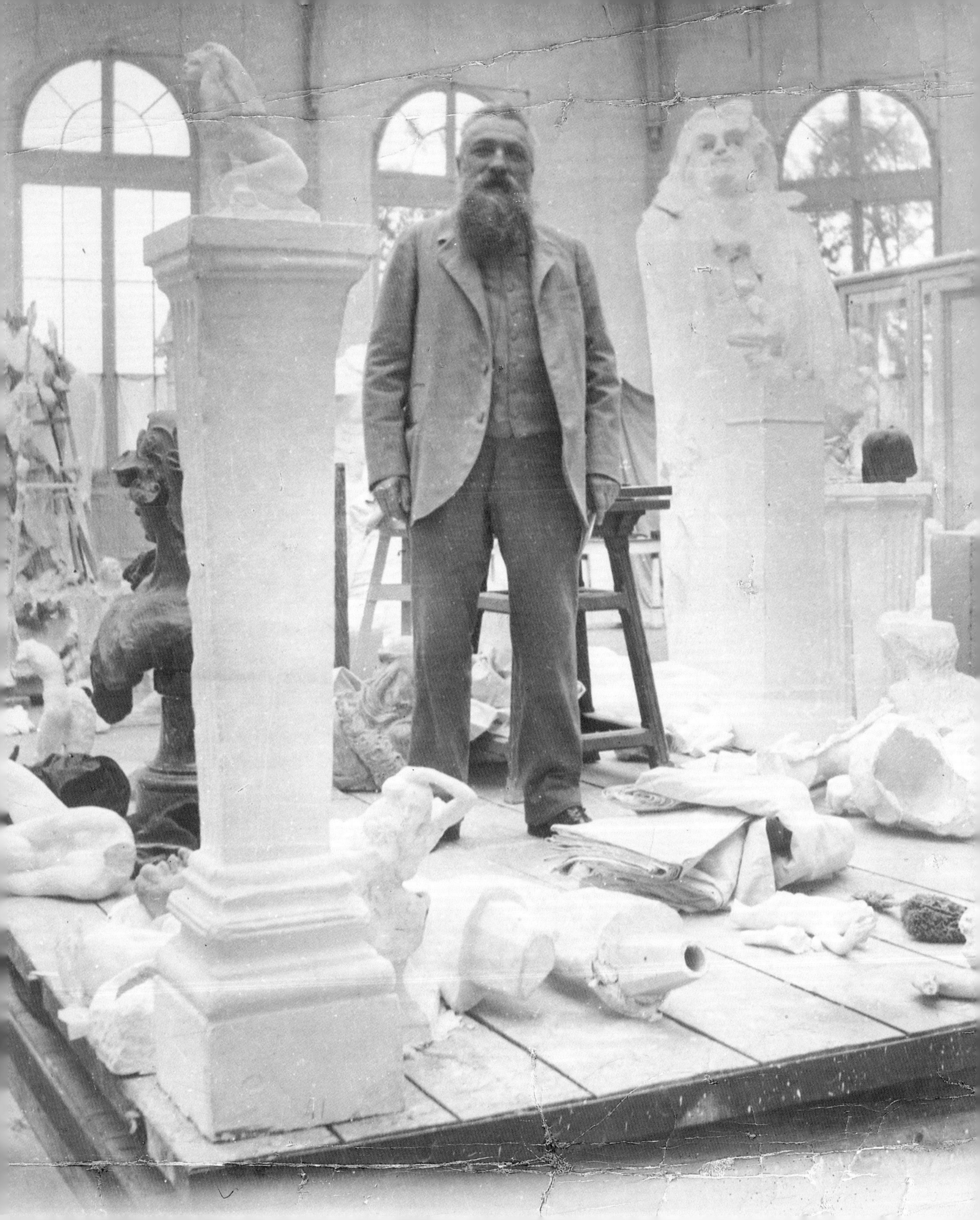

Techniques

Drawing was of central importance to Rodin's practice, as he once revealed by his comment, 'It's quite simple, my drawings are the key to my work.' Rodin often started a sculpture by sketching life models from many different angles, including from above while balanced on a stepladder. Using a technique sometimes referred to as 'blind drawing', he drew quickly, without taking his eyes away from the model in front of him, his aim being to depict exactly what he saw. These drawings helped him to understand the forms he was about to sculpt.

Although a finished sculpture may be made from bronze, stone or marble, Rodin first sculpted his creations in clay. On sculptures that have later been cast in bronze, we can often find his fingerprints and other marks that were embedded into the surface of the clay original, reminding us of the pliable, soft material that was worked by the artist. From the clay sculpture, Rodin would create a mould, from which a plaster cast could be made. Rodin often made several initial plaster casts. Keeping several of the same plaster casts allowed him flexibility: he could return to them and try out various changes. These plaster casts were treated as the original models for a design. Unlike clay, which would have to be kept wet and was therefore difficult to preserve, plaster casts could be kept for a long time. They could be used as the model from which a marble sculpture could be copied, or could be used to create moulds from which many bronze versions could be cast.

Opposite: Photographs of Rodin at work show that his studio was filled with fragments, plaster casts and bronzes, often at different stages of production. Auguste Rodin in his studio in Meudon, 1902. Musée Rodin, Paris, Ph.203.

This way, Rodin could repeat the bronze casting process many times over, and at different times, matching demand for his sculpture.

When casting a sculpture in bronze, Rodin worked with foundries – companies who specialized in this process – to create either sand or lost-wax casts. The two processes go back thousands of years. They produce a similar effect but with a few key differences. Sand casting, the more common process, involves a plaster cast pressed into sand, creating an imprint from which a bronze cast can then be made. Lost-wax casting is a more complicated, time-consuming and expensive process, involving molten metal replacing a concrete-encased wax model of the original clay or plaster sculpture.

The varying properties of the two techniques made them useful to Rodin for different reasons. The lost-wax process, for example, allowed Rodin to work on his design during the process of casting, by carving directly into the wax model. He favoured the technique for experimental projects such as *The Gates of Hell*. Sand casting, on the other hand, did not allow for these last-minute changes. The technique produced an impression very faithful to the original, which was useful for Rodin as a number of his designs were reproduced by foundries in large quantities. Another difference relates to the original model used to make the cast. The sand-casting process meant that the plaster model would be damaged in the process, often with parts cut off and cast separately. The lost-wax process, however, did not harm the original clay or plaster model in any way. In fact, it actually strengthened it. *The Duchess of Choiseul* is a rare example of a sculpture made using the lost-wax technique.

When creating marble versions of his sculptures, Rodin worked with specialists who transferred his designs from bronze or plaster to marble. Rodin was involved in the transferral, making marks on the marble in chalk or pencil to guide his assistants in the carving process. Sometimes Rodin's bronzes were cast from a marble original, rather than from one of bronze, plaster or clay. This is the case for *Fleeting Love.*

Rodin's sculptures were sometimes enlarged or reduced to fit different purposes, for example large public monuments, or small sculptures to show domestically. For this purpose, he used a system devised in 1836 by the French engineer Achille Collas (1795–1859). The invention of the Collas machine was inspired by a pantograph, an instrument for copying a plan or drawing to a different scale. The Collas machine connected two turntables, one featuring the object to be enlarged or reduced, and the other a lump of clay. As a tracing needle moved across the original, the design was carved with a sharp instrument on to the piece of clay. Rodin worked with the sculptor Henri Lebossé (1856–1922), who dedicated himself to enlarging Rodin's designs. The process was exhausting: at one point, Lebosse was working from 6am until midnight on an enlargement of Rodin's *The Thinker*, telling the artist he hoped to be his 'perfect collaborator'.

In later years Rodin developed a fascinating technique called 'assemblage'. Throughout his career, the artist amassed a large collection of his own plaster casts, including individual limbs in various poses, and heads with different expressions. He reused these works in different combinations, forming new sculptures. *The Wave* was made using this technique.

When Rodin died, responsibility for his casts and for managing the authorization of copies passed to the Musée Rodin.

Opposite: Referred to by the artist as his *'abattis'* ('giblets'), Rodin created a large collection of sculpted body parts which he could reuse to make new sculptures. Sculptured body parts, Auguste Rodin. Musée Rodin, Paris.

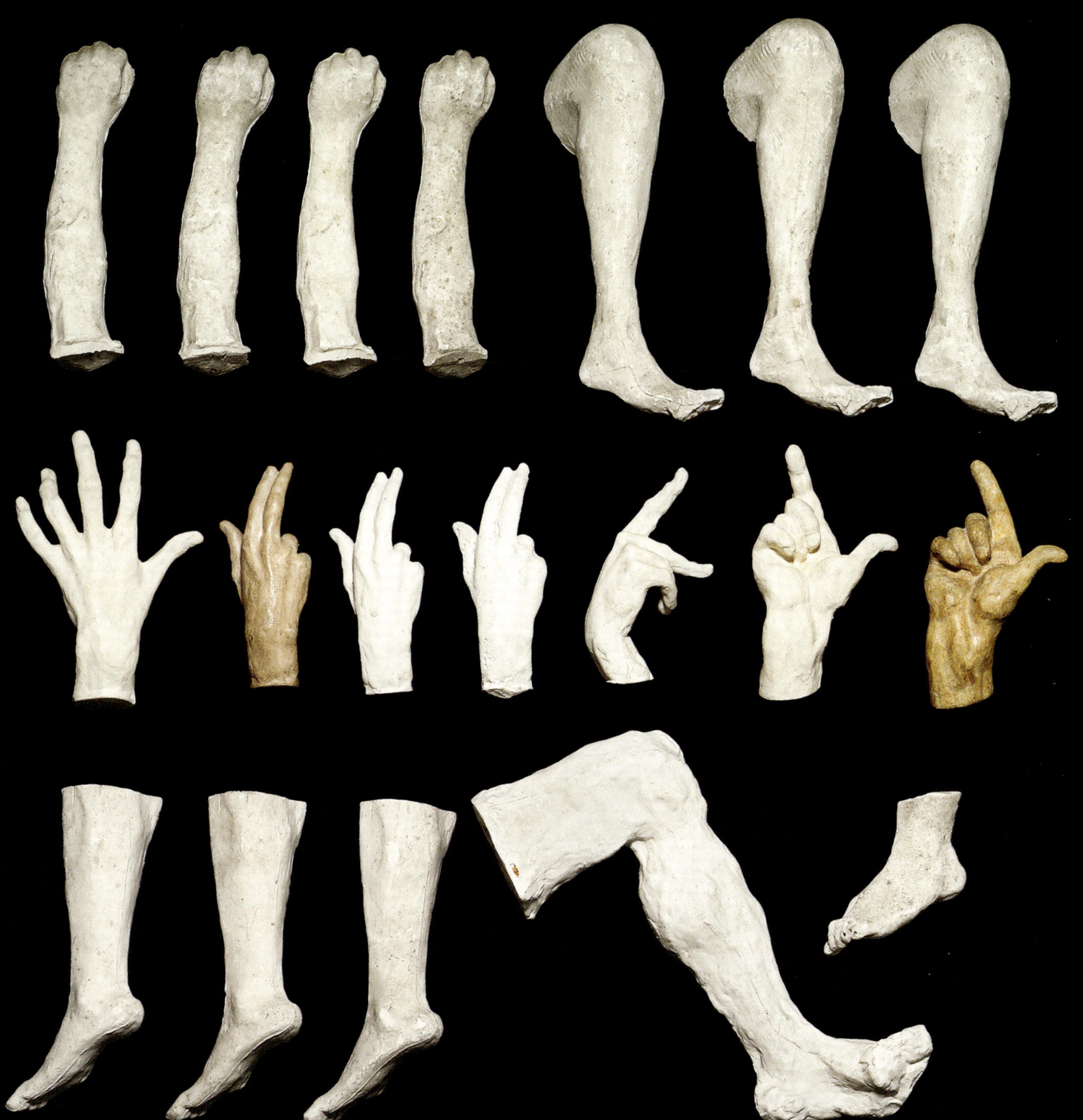

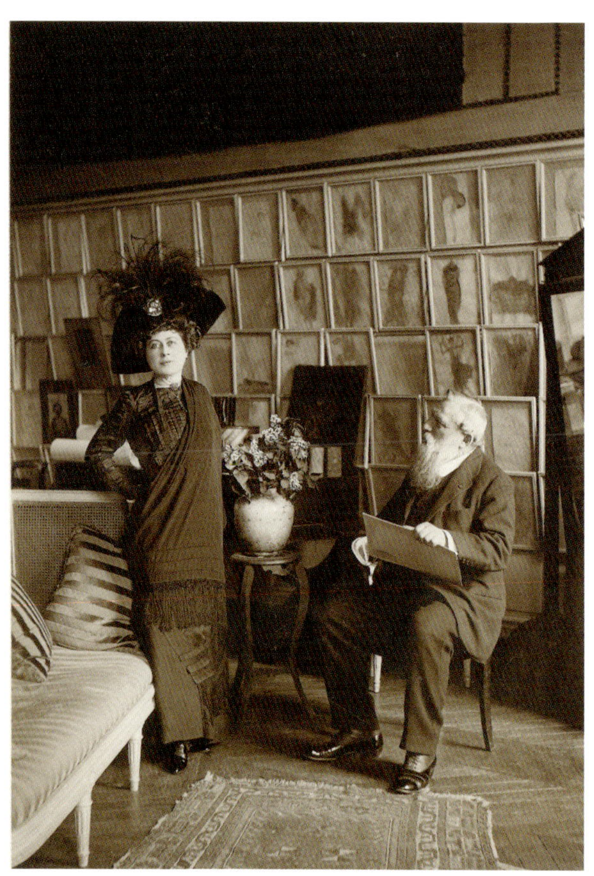

Claire Coudert and Rodin often met at the Hôtel Biron, where they liked to listen to records on a gramophone Rodin bought for Coudert. Auguste Rodin and Claire Coudert at the Hôtel Biron, Paris, around 1909. Musée Rodin, Paris,

The Duchess of Choiseul, 1908

Cast in bronze by Montagutelli, before 1923
Bronze
35.8 x 35.3 x 19.4 cm
7.15

Claire Coudert (1864–1919) was Rodin's last great lover. She came into Rodin's life around 1904, full of vitality and 24 years his junior. Coudert, who became a duchess around the time this sculpture was made, played a role in Rodin's life that no other woman did, taking control of his business dealings and increasing the value of his sculptures through shrewd management.

Rodin and Coudert's love affair ended in 1912, after she was said to be exerting too much control over the artist, cutting him off from his friends. She is even said to have once exclaimed, 'I handle everything. I am Rodin!'

Rodin's sculptures of Claire Coudert were not commissioned, instead they were inspired by the pair's close relationship. The artist sculpted her portrait twice: in one of these she is shown laughing; here, she seems about to speak.

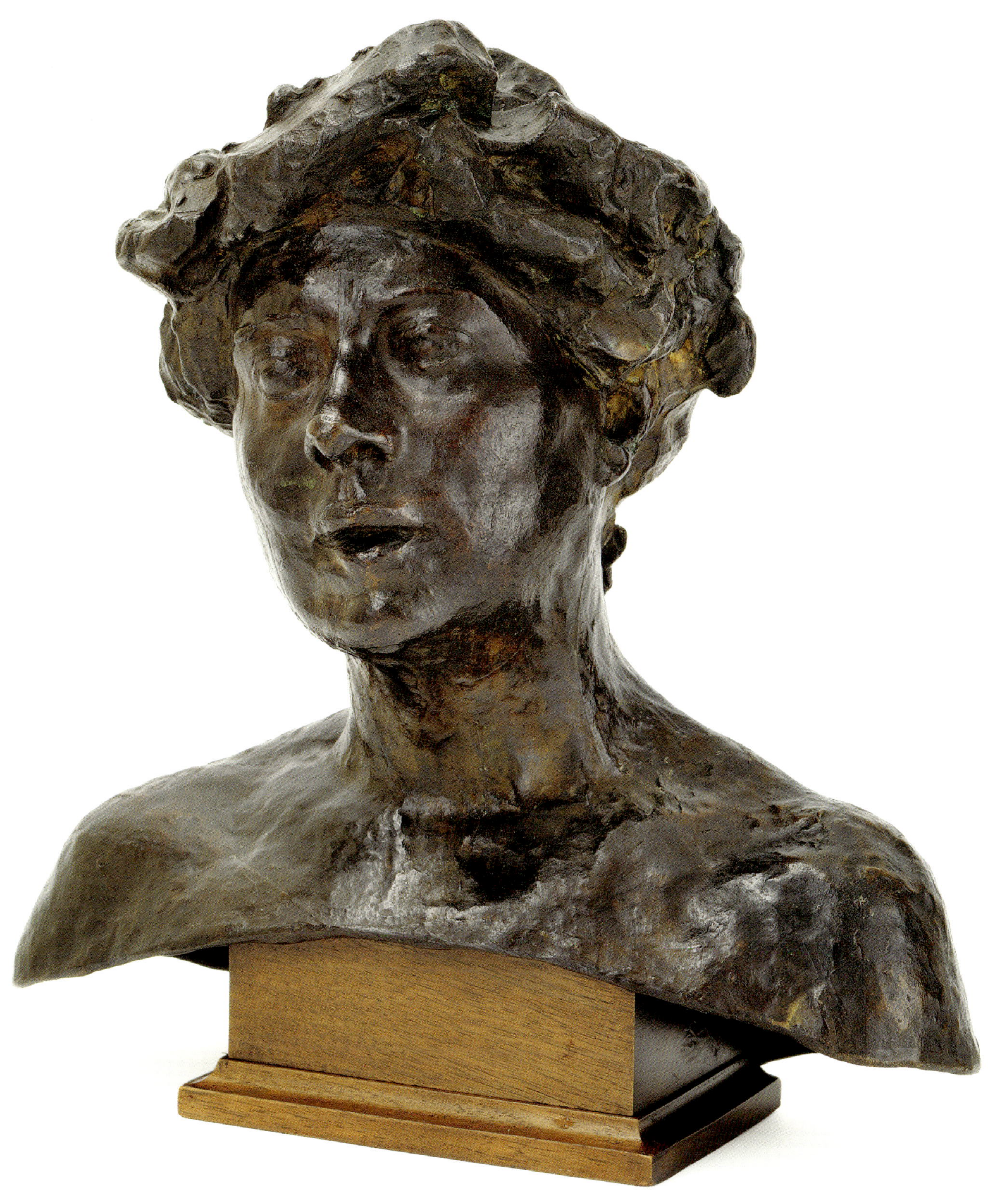

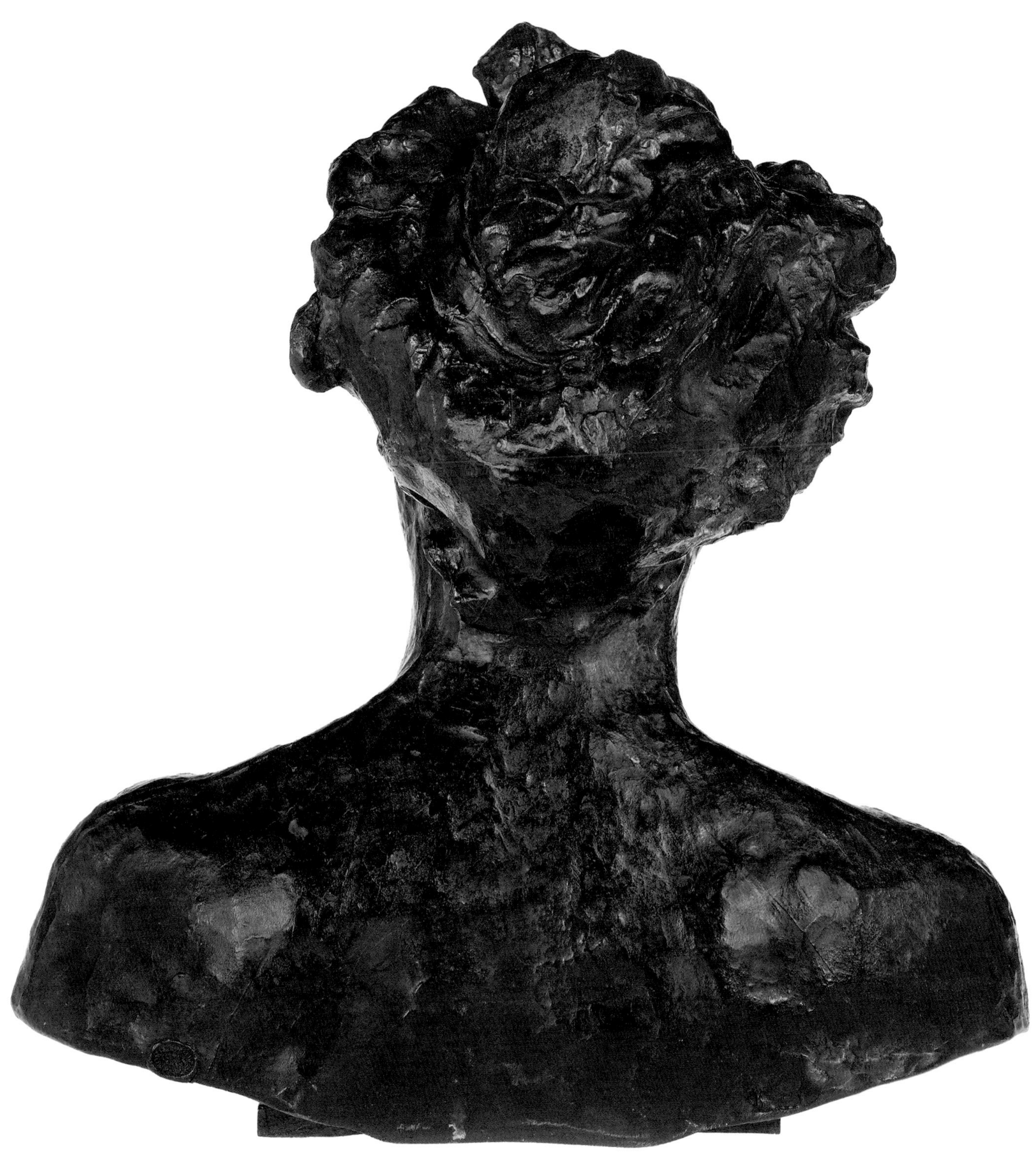

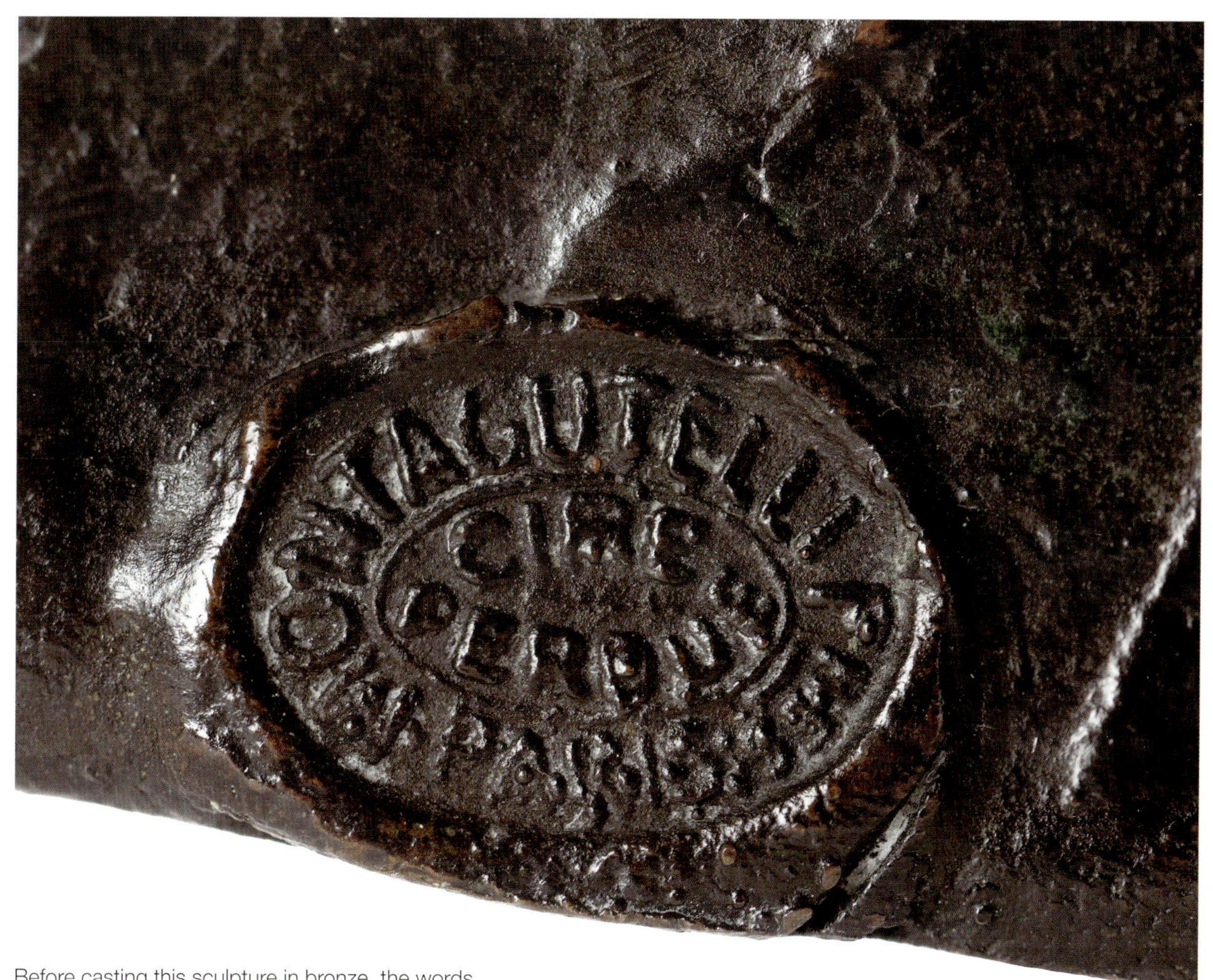

Before casting this sculpture in bronze, the words
'CIRE PERDUE' ('lost wax') were stamped into the surface
of the wax model. This can be found at the back of the
sculpture, towards the left.

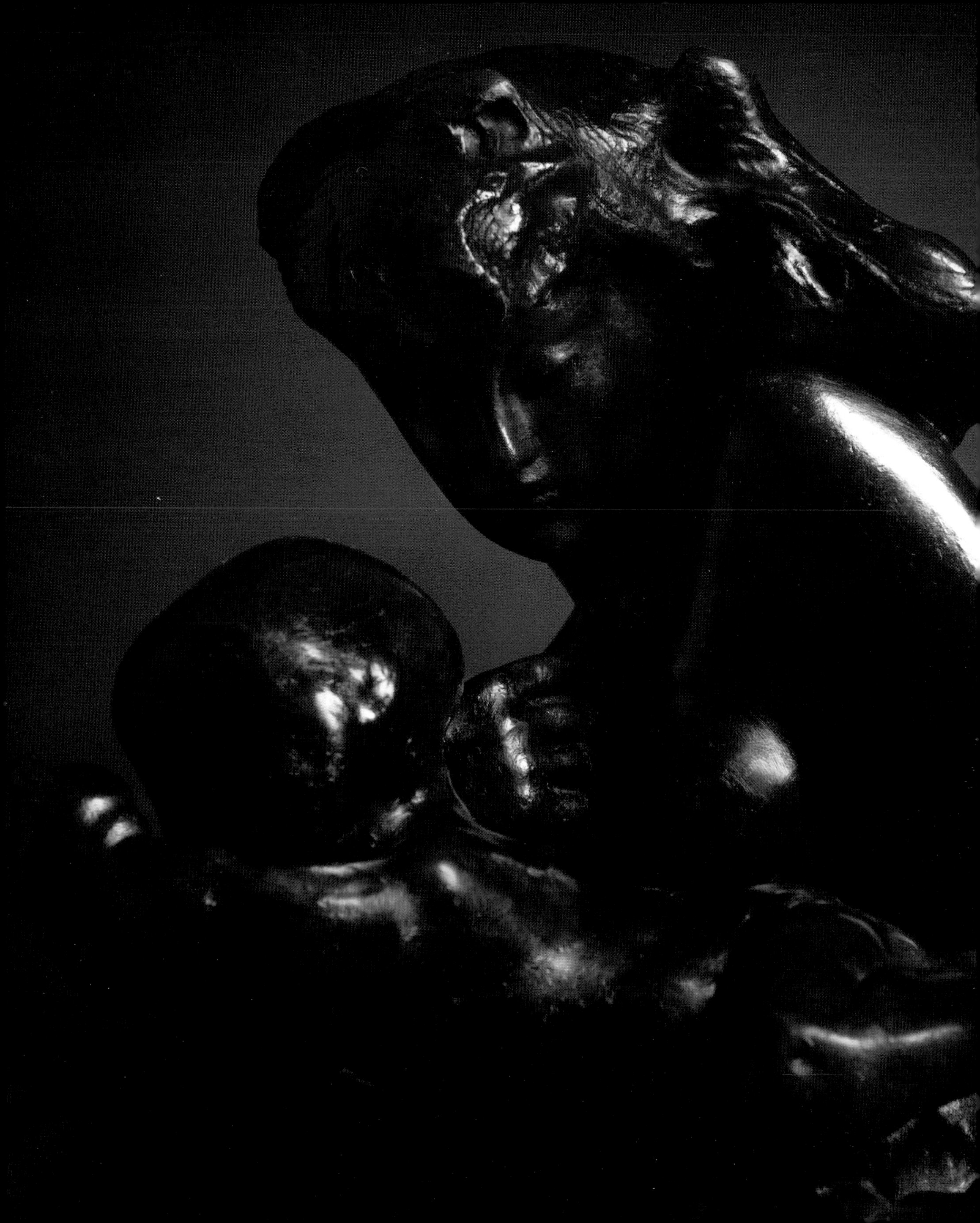

Fleeting Love, 1885
Cast in bronze before 1911
Bronze
38.7 x 36 x 26.5 cm
7.11

In the 1880s Rodin made three small sculptures on the theme of maternal love. Each sculpture is a variation of the same design of a seated woman with a child at her knee. *Fleeting Love* is one of these three, the remaining two being close variations of *Mother and Child in the Grotto* (pp. 28–29). In *Fleeting Love*, the young woman holds a child who stretches out on her lap. Rodin has charmingly transformed the infant into a cherub by adding two small wings.

This sculpture was cast from an original that was made from marble, rather than plaster, clay or bronze. The scratchy marks detailing the figures' hair, as well as those seen on the base, match the marks on Rodin's marble sculpture. Often his marbles feature very smooth sections alongside areas which have many visible scratches and other marks left by the carving tools.

This sculpture is one of the earliest Rodins to have been purchased by William Burrell. It was probably bought in the early 1890s through Alexander Reid, the progressive Scottish art dealer, and may have been the sculpture Burrell lent to the 1901 Glasgow International Exhibition (see p. 29).

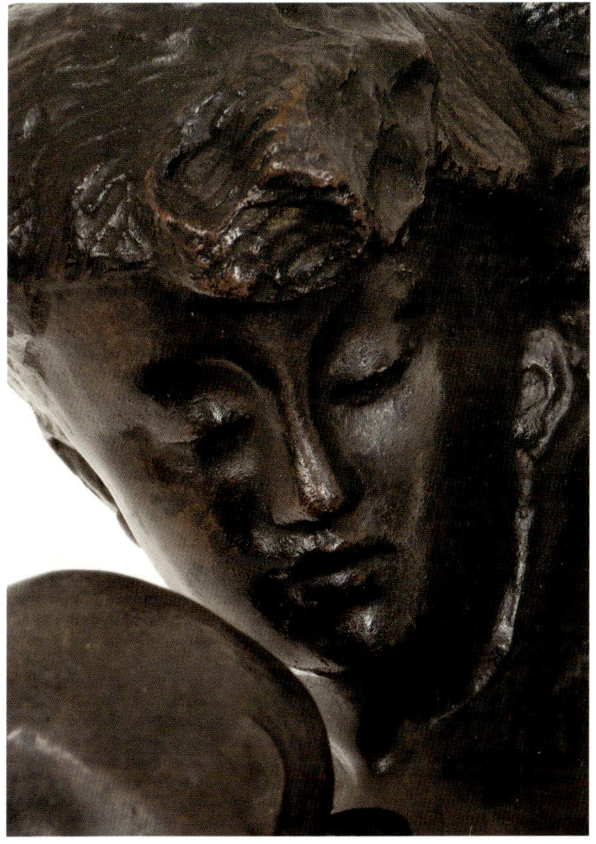

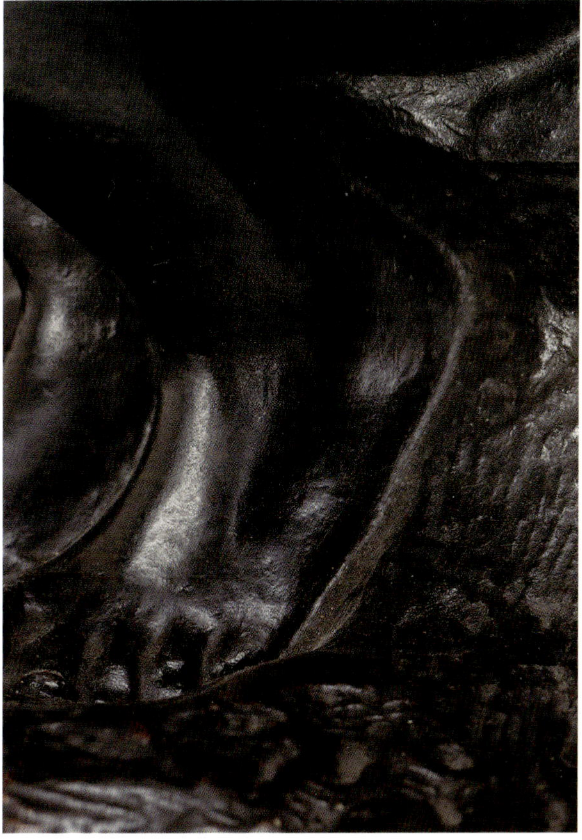

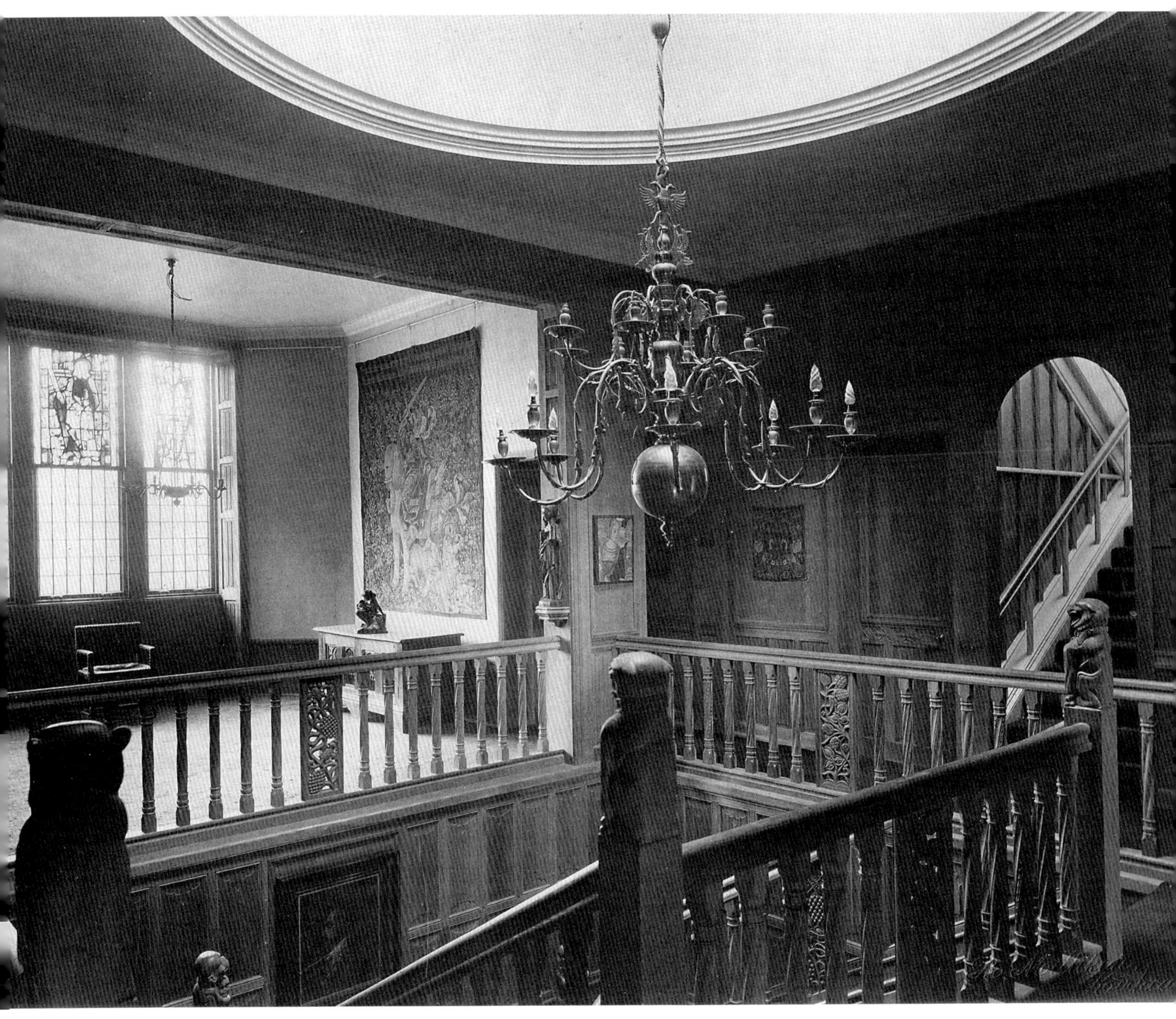

William and Constance Burrell's townhouse in Glasgow's West End was full of their collection. Here *Fleeting Love* – at the time a piece of contemporary art – can be seen on an ornate wooden table, underneath a medieval tapestry. The staircase of 8 Great Western Terrace, 1902, by R Miliken. Glasgow Museums Archive, 52.40.1.18.

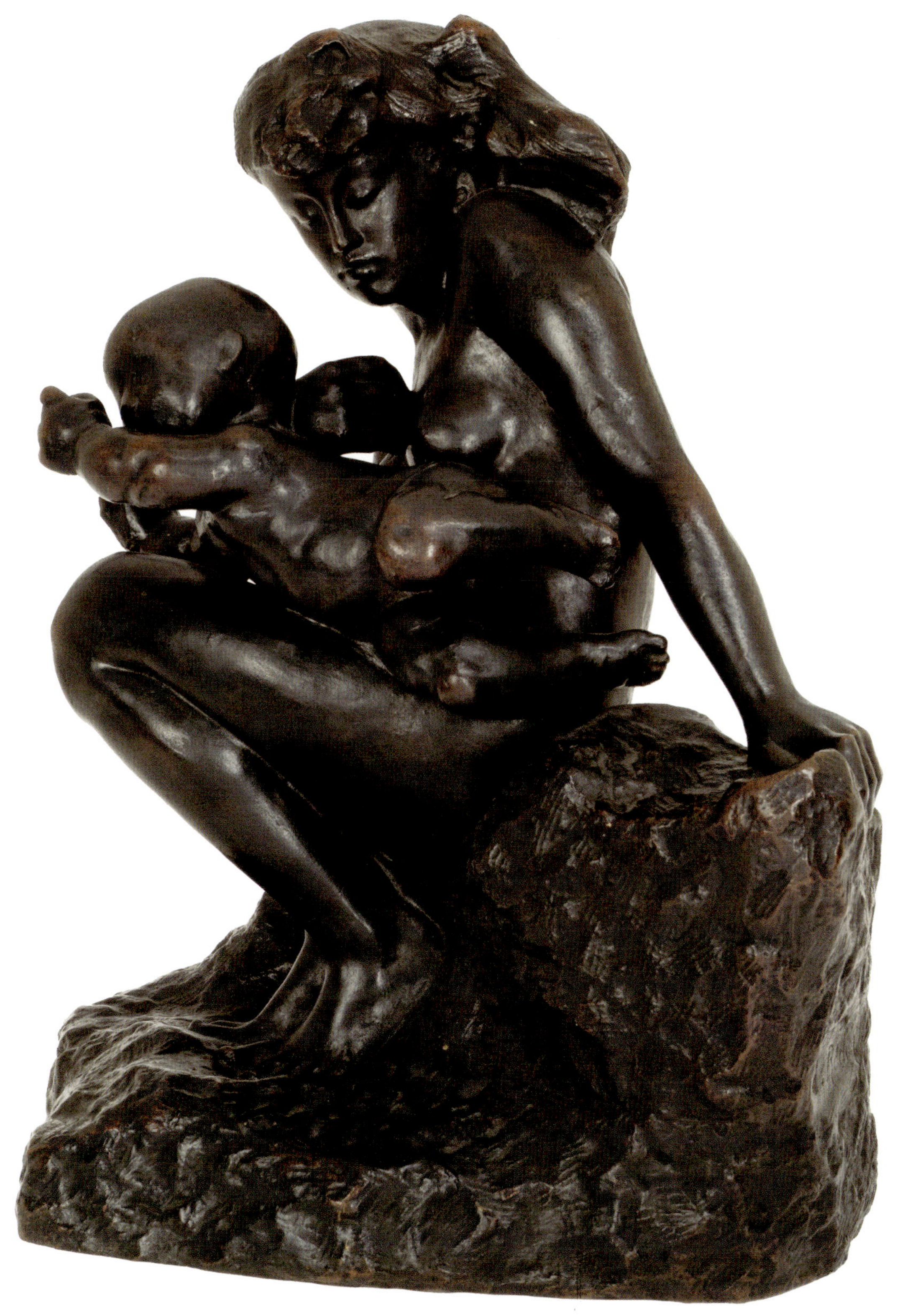

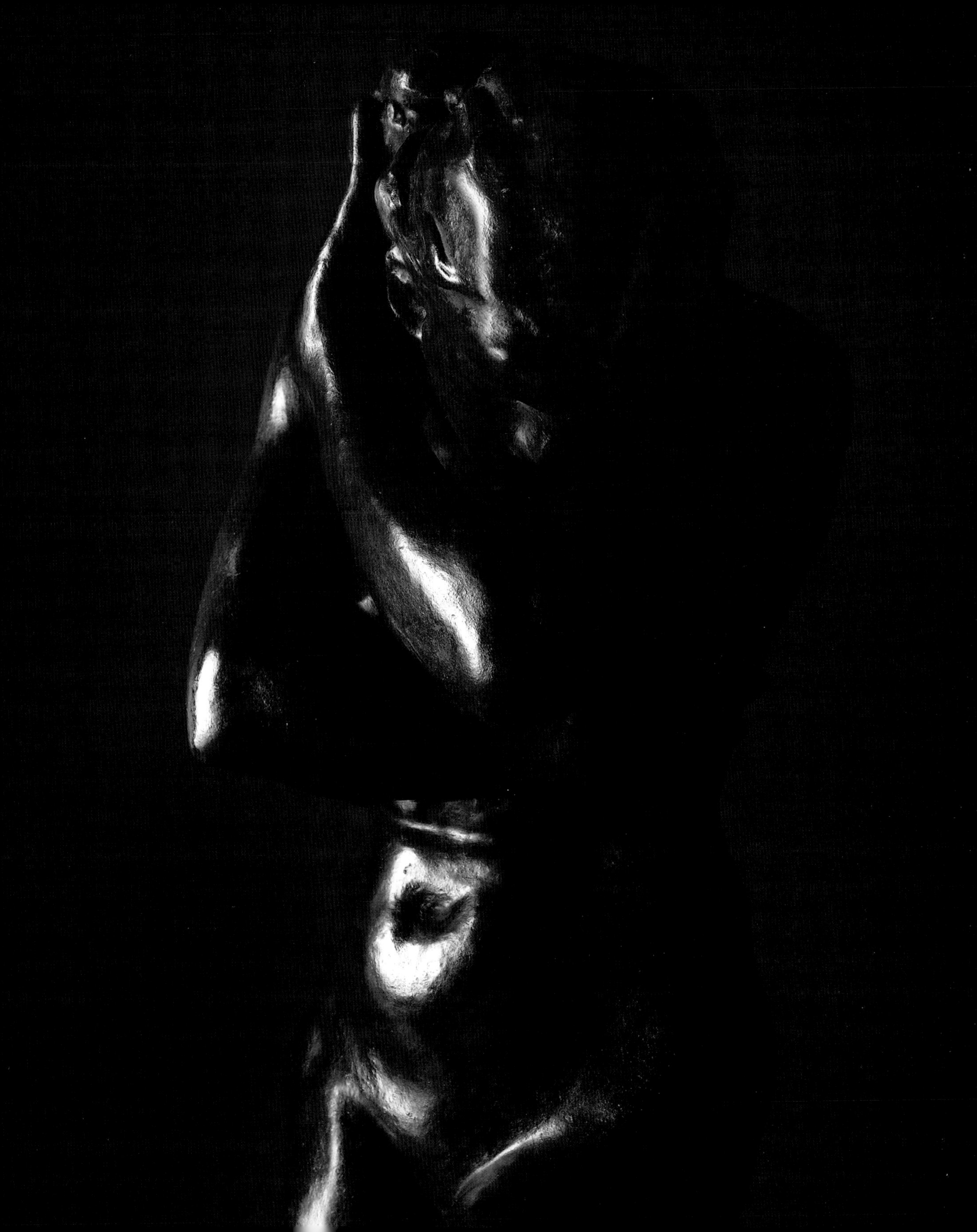

Eve After the Fall, 1882–83

Cast in bronze by Alexis Rudier Foundry, 1903–17
Bronze
75 x 45 x 42 cm
7.12

In 1881 Rodin started a life size sculpture of Eve,
intended for *The Gates of Hell* (see pp. 26–27).
He abandoned that design temporarily, and instead
focused his attentions on a smaller version.

As with other sculptors working at the time, when
Rodin organized a reduction or enlargement of his
sculptures, these were usually made using a Collas
machine, a system involving the reproduction of
a sculpture through tracing needles and rotating
turntables (see p. 42). This produced a reduction
or enlargement that was incredibly close to the
original, albeit of a different size. The version we see
here, however, is not entirely faithful to the original.
Details such as the angle of Eve's head, her hair,
left hand and left foot are in different positions,
while areas like her buttocks appear more rounded,
and her waist more curvaceous. Furthermore, the
surface of the smaller *Eve* appears smoother and
more carefully modelled. These variations from
the original could be explained by the fact that,
when he started work on the smaller *Eve*, Rodin
was not working from a sculpture he considered
to be finished and ready for exact reproduction. It
is possible that, rather than reducing his life-sized
Eve using the Collas technique, Rodin modelled an
entirely new version. Its small size and appealing
sensuality made it very popular amongst collectors,
and there were dozens of casts made which are
today to be found in collections around the world.

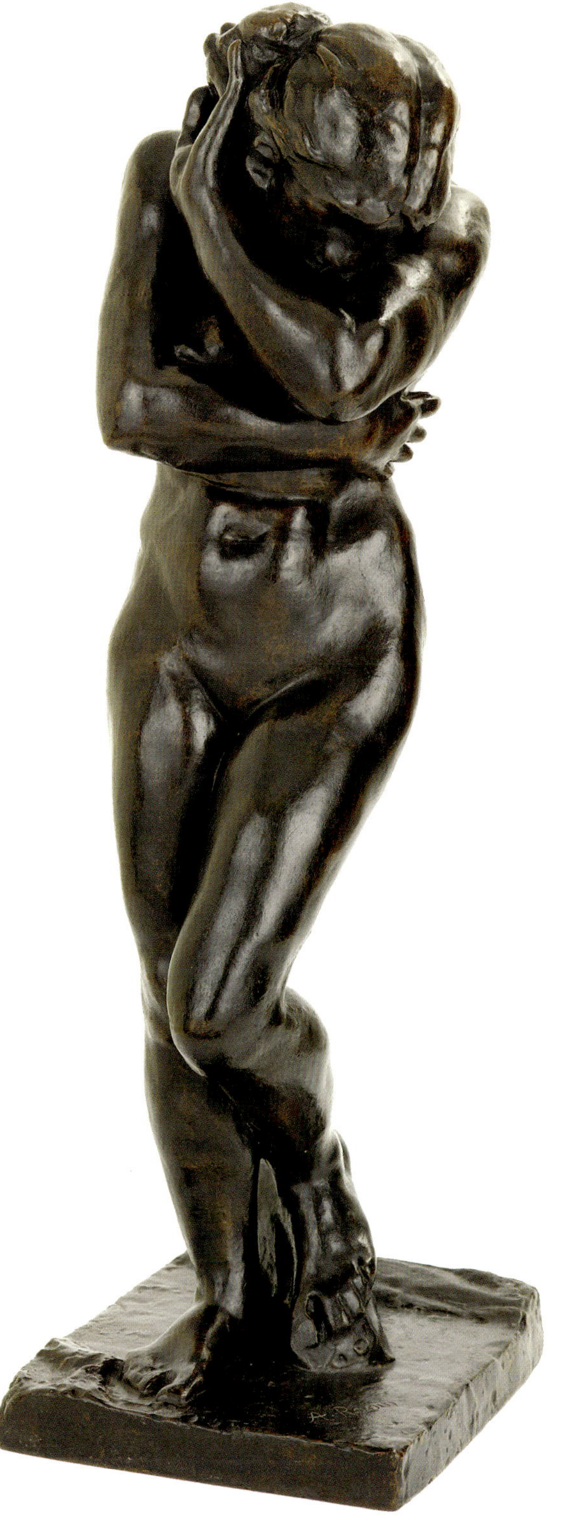

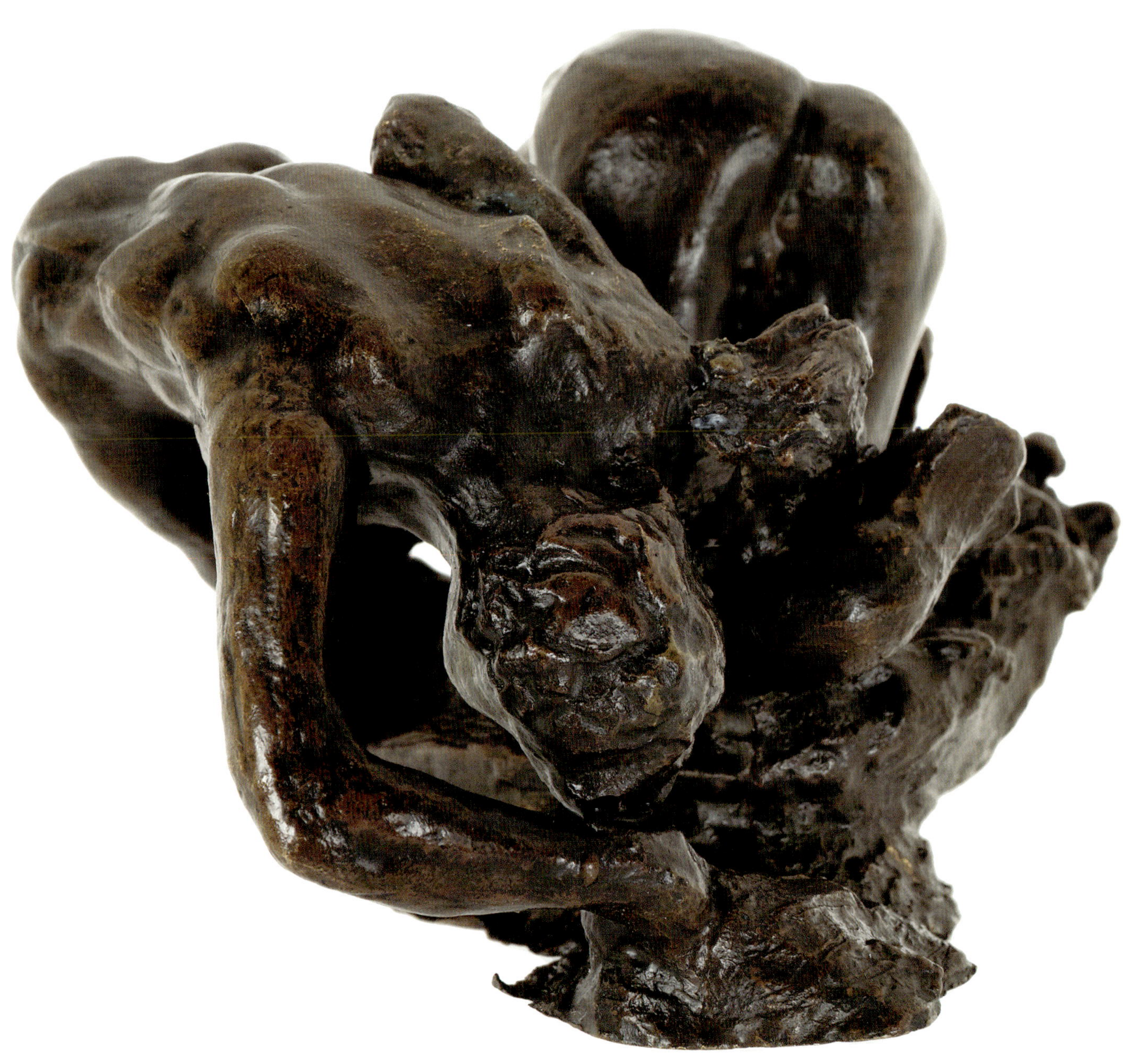

The Wave, about 1885–1900
Cast in bronze by Léon Perzinka, 1896–1900
Bronze
10.6 x 25 x 15.2 cm
7.9

Sirens, according to classical mythology, lured sailors to their watery deaths through haunting song. They became an enduring motif of temptation and ruin, featuring in the writing of both Homer and Ovid, who described three sirens as the handmaids of Persephone, goddess of the underworld. The theme of sirens and the sea clearly intrigued Rodin, for he sculpted a small series of figures on this theme in the 1880s. Around 1887, he included a group of three sirens in _The Gates of Hell_, and also later incorporated the group into his _Monument to Victor Hugo,_ Palais-Royal, Paris.

In this small sculpture, two bodies twist and turn in frothy waves. The male figure reaches ahead, as if trying to pull himself forward, whereas the female figure seems to dive into the waves, her head dipping below the surface. She has small, fin-like growths instead of arms, and her legs seem to twist into a tail-like shape, giving her the identity of a mythical siren.

The Wave is a unique cast, meaning that there are no other examples of this design to be found anywhere in the world today. This is unusual, as Rodin would normally arrange for a bronze sculpture to be cast numerous times. It is an example of the artist's 'assemblage' technique, where he would take different parts of existing sculptures and arrange them in new ways. The female figure in _The Wave_ can be found, albeit slightly altered, in a number of other sculptures by the artist, including held in a 1917 life cast of Rodin's hand.

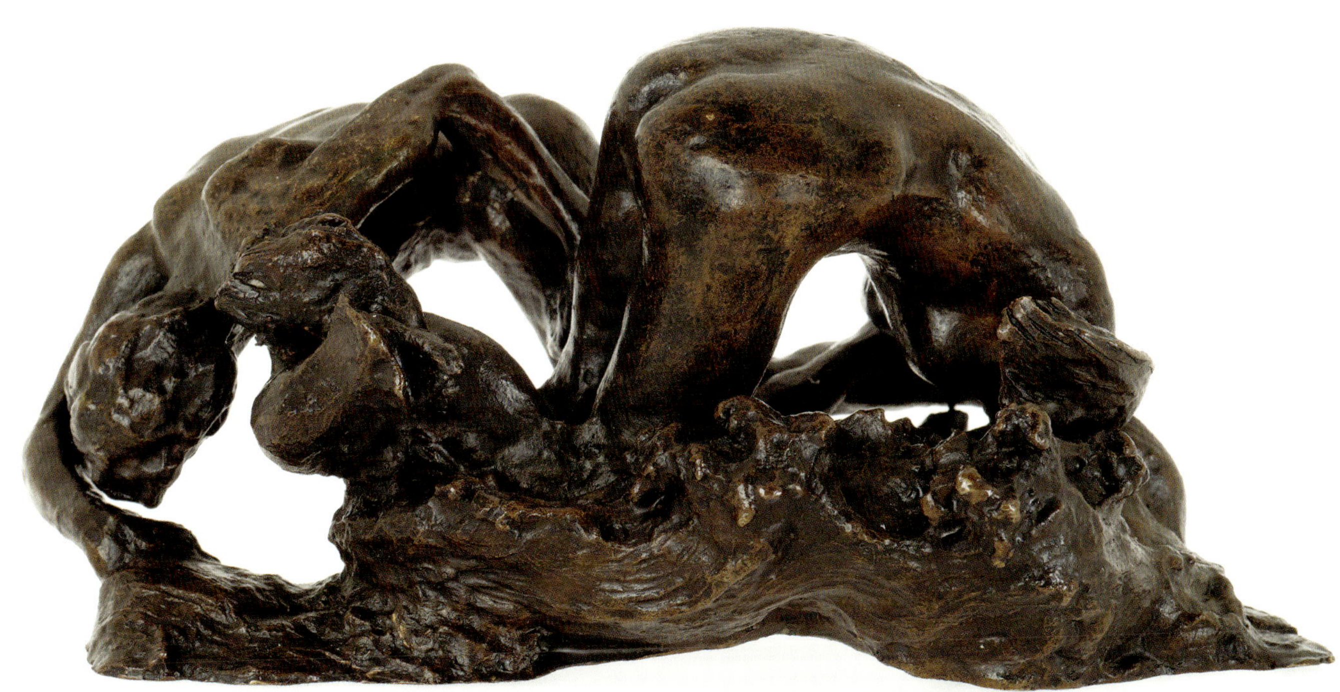

When a bronze cast is completed, it is normally hollow. Unusually, as this view from below shows, *The Wave* is filled with a white material. Photographs of the sculpture from when it was exhibited in 1900 do not show the white core, so it seems it was added at a later date. Remnants of a sticky green substance on the bottom suggest that it was once covered with felt, which may have protected the surface upon which it sat. The white core may have been added to give the sculpture a more stable base, or to provide a support for the green felt.

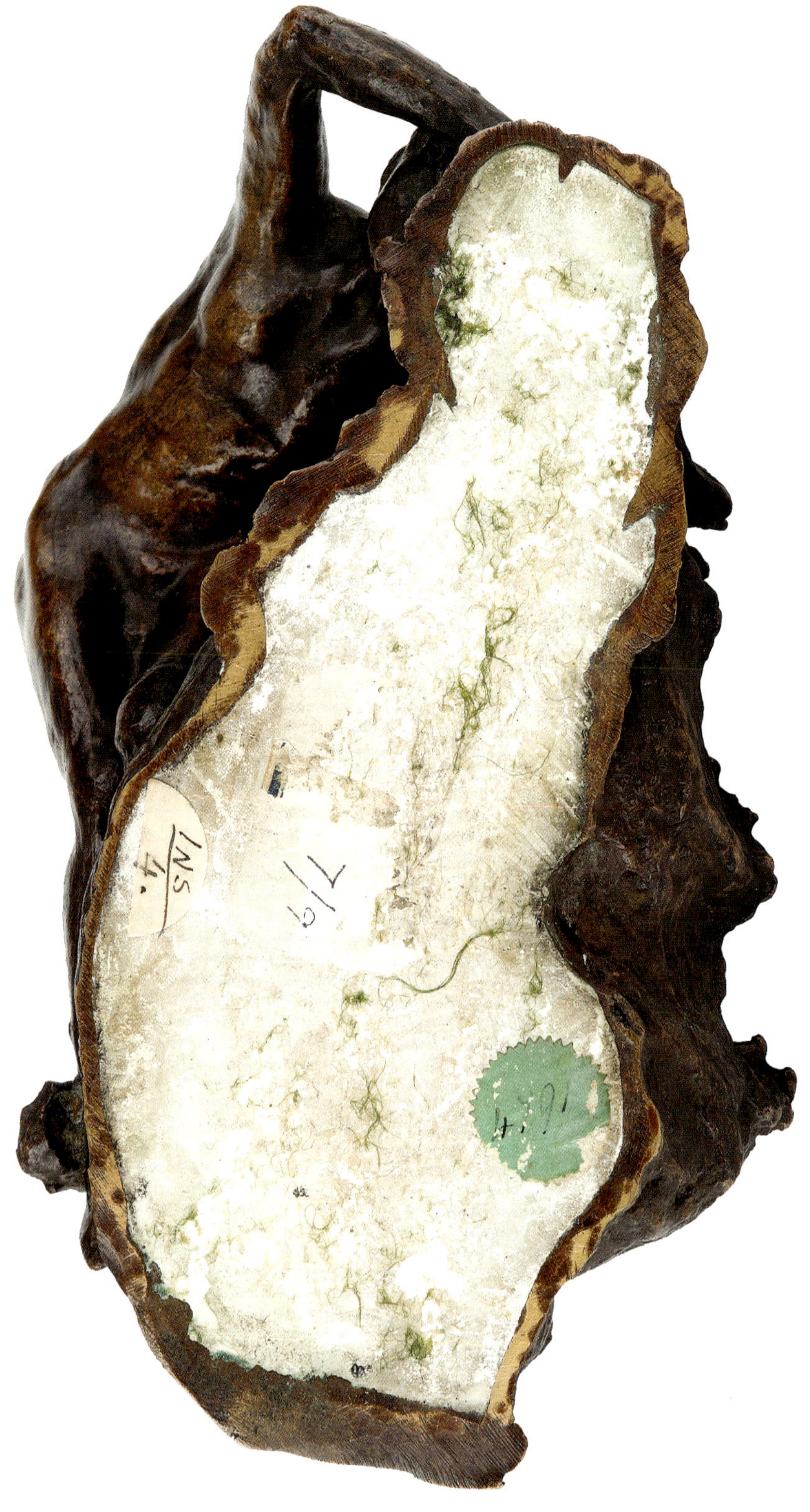

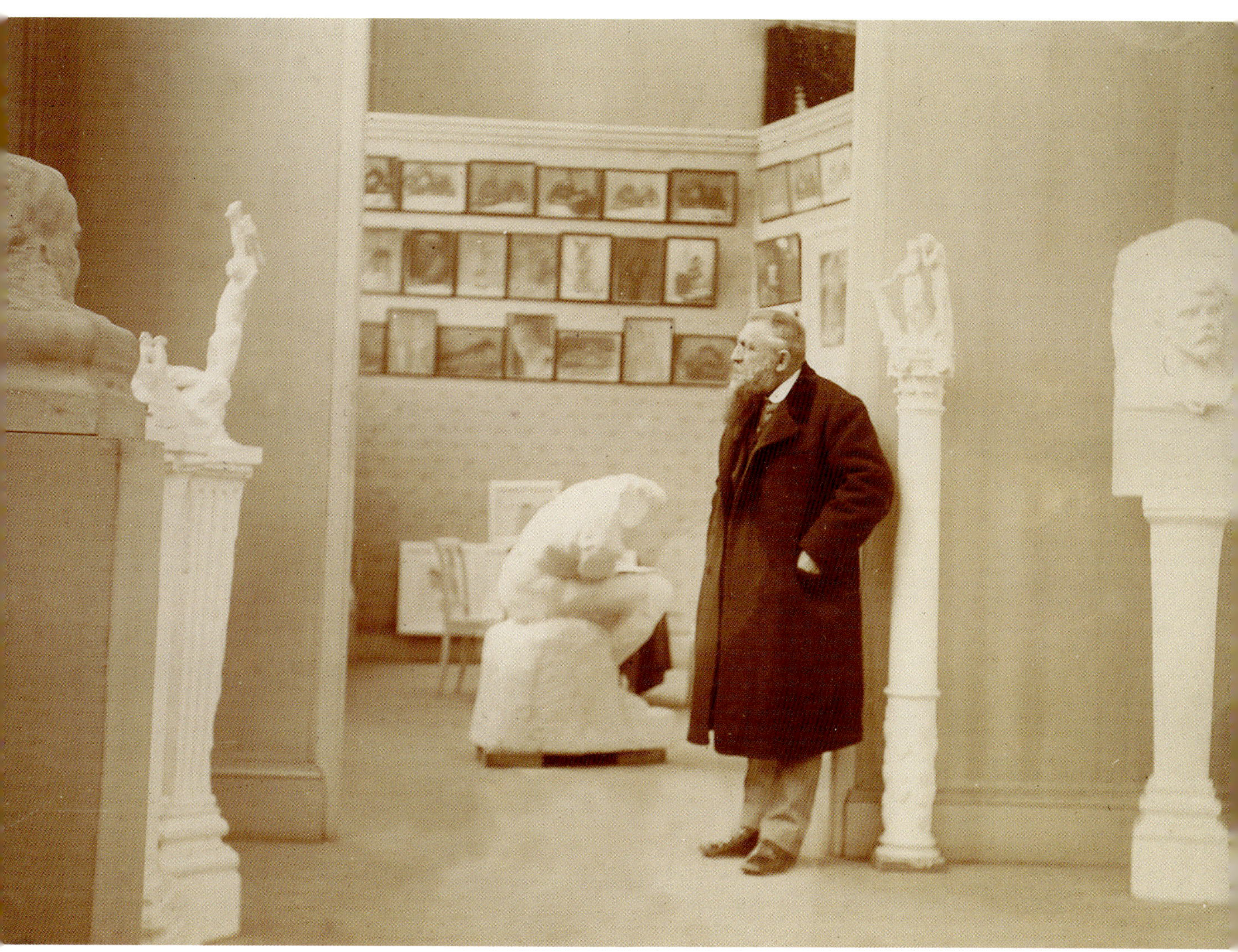

In his first solo exhibition, in 1900, Rodin displayed nine framed photographs of *The Wave*, which showed the sculpture from different angles. Here they can be seen in the upper row of photographs on the walls of one of the exhibition rooms. Auguste Rodin at the Pavillon de l'Alma, Paris, 1900, by M Bauche. Musée Rodin, Paris, Ph.790.

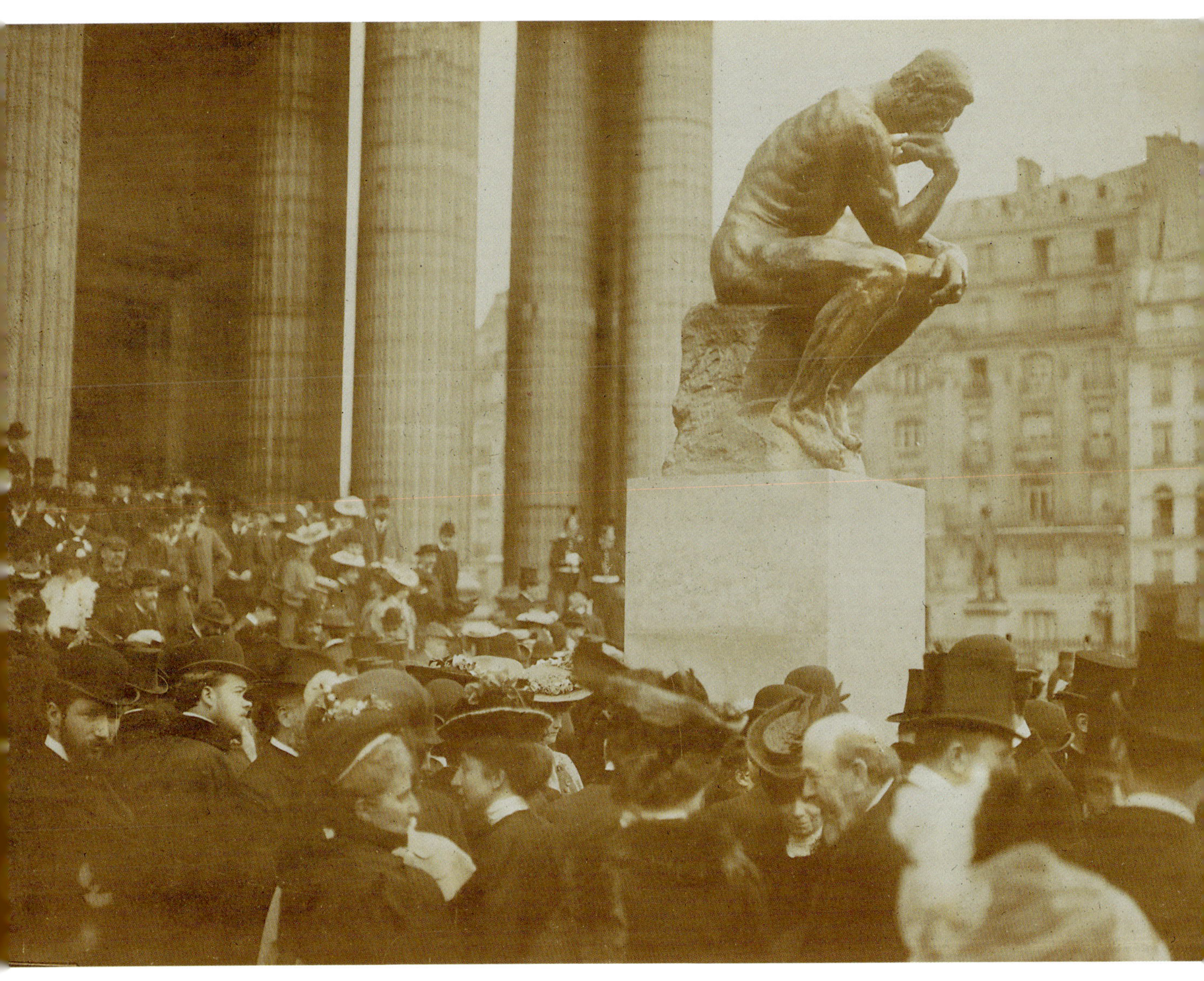

The placement of *The Thinker* close to the Panthéon, Paris, where France's most important citizens, including Victor Hugo, were interred, was hugely significant for Rodin. His genius was at last publicly recognized by his native city. *The Thinker* in front of the Panthéon, Paris, 1906. Musée Rodin, Paris, Ph.754.

Monuments

Monuments played an important role in France during Rodin's lifetime. For the new Third Republic, beginning in 1870 after a century of political upheaval, sculptures in marble, stone or bronze served to suggest the stability of the fledgling state. It commissioned three times as many monuments as previous French regimes, including ones to decorate public buildings in the newly enlarged Paris, which had grown in the preceding two decades during the reign of Emperor Napoleon III (1803–73), incorporating eight more *arrondissements* (administrative districts).

Monuments also played a vital role for sculptors. Perhaps even more important than exhibiting in the annual Paris Salon exhibition, winning a commission for a public monument was a route to success. Along with receiving a fee, the prestige could make a sculptor's reputation.

Although Rodin submitted ideas for monuments, a number of these were rejected. Both his 1879 model for a statue to mark the defence of Paris, and his design for the town hall of the thirteenth *arrondissement* failed to reach the second stage of the competition, probably because they contained aspects appearing too aggressive, failing to match the image that the Republic was seeking to project.

Monuments to commemorate notable people sprang up frequently in France during the nineteenth century, a time of important visual artists and literary luminaries. Rodin personally admired many of these individuals, and it must have been an honour to sculpt in their memory. The artist received several commissions for memorials, including a monument to Victor Hugo (1802–85), another to Charles Baudelaire (1821–67) and a third to Honoré de Balzac (1799–1850) – all important writers who greatly inspired Rodin. None of these monuments went to plan: the sculpture for Hugo was seen as unsuitable for its intended position at the prestigious Panthéon, from 1881 used exclusively as a mausoleum for prominent French citizens, and instead it was moved to the gardens of the Palais-Royal, where it was finally unveiled in 1909. Rodin was asked to try again with his design of a statue for the Panthéon: this new sculpture, *The Apotheosis of Victor Hugo*, progressed no further than the second maquette, Rodin eventually losing interest. The monument to Baudelaire failed to gain support from a public appeal, and therefore Rodin got no further with his plans for an ambitious monument to the writer than modelling a series of studies representing Baudelaire's head. Rodin's long project to commemorate Balzac was harshly rejected by the commissioning Société des Gens de Lettres, and was ridiculed in the French press.

Other sculptures by Rodin did appear as monuments in a few cities across France. The first was his memorial to the painter Jules Bastien-Lepage (1848–84), unveiled in 1889. His colossal sculpture *The Burghers of Calais* was unveiled in Calais in 1895. However, Rodin still dreamt of his sculpture being viewed on the streets of his native Paris. It was not until 1906 that a public monument by the artist was permanently installed in the capital, an enlarged *The Thinker*, which was paid for by public subscription.

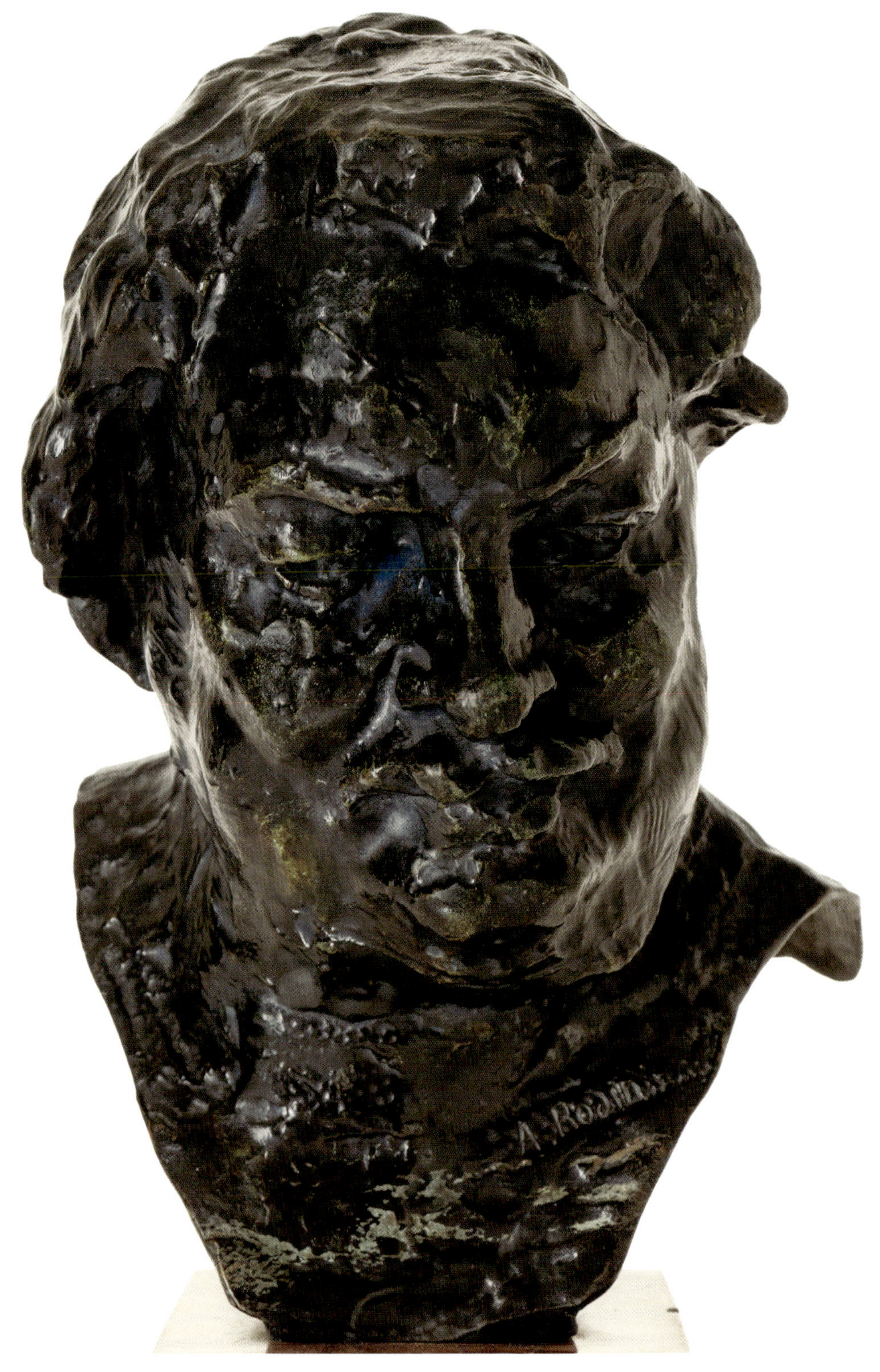

Balzac, 1892–93
Cast in bronze by Alexis Rudier Foundry, 1918–20
Bronze
28.2 x 19 x 22.2 cm
7.16

When Rodin received a commission in 1891
from the Société des Gens de Lettres, a French
association of writers, he started work immediately.
He was to make a monument to Honoré de Balzac,
the famous novelist and playwright. It took him
seven years of careful study, during which he
created 50 preparatory sculptures, and even visited
the region Balzac came from to observe the faces
of locals.

One of Rodin's preparatory sculptures included a
full-length nude sculpture of Balzac, made in
1892–93, which showed the writer standing with
his legs apart, arms folded defiantly (p. 62). The
Société judged it too unflattering, requesting a
younger and slimmer Balzac. Rodin still cast the
naked Balzac figure in bronze for his collectors. He
also used the head of the nude *Balzac* to make
busts, such as this example in the Burrell Collection.

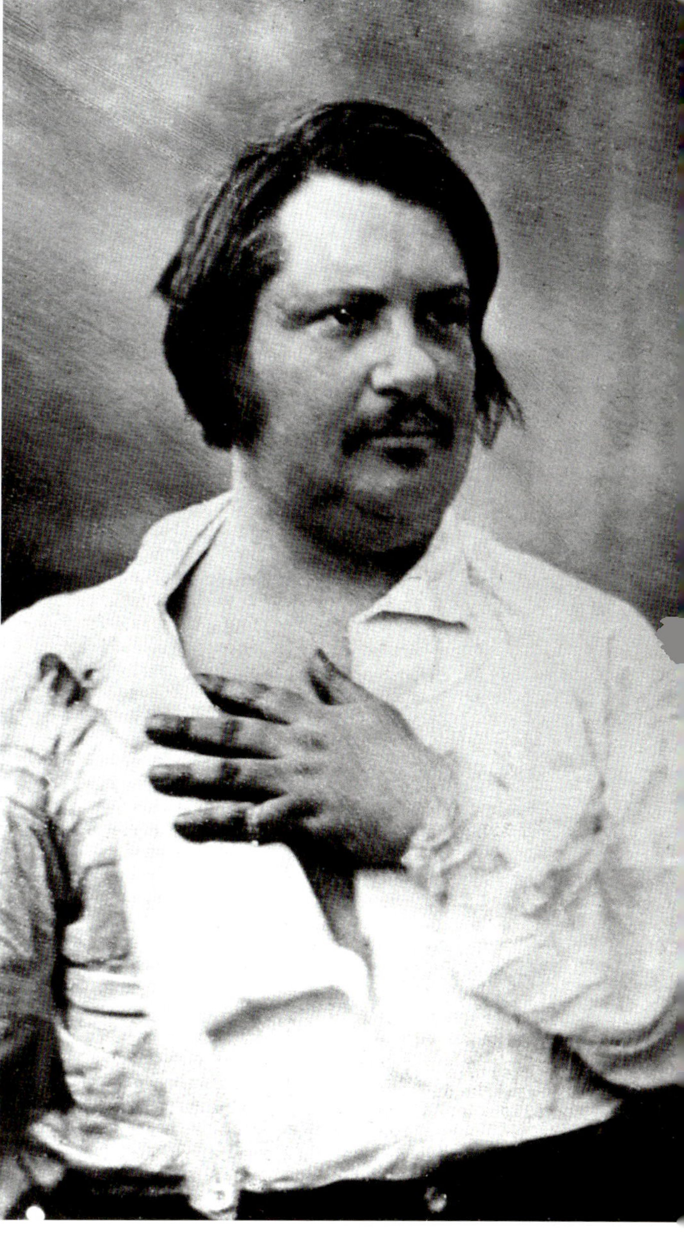

Rodin acknowledged the great writer Balzac's unkempt
appearance, commenting, 'Balzac should have had a woman
to take care of him and to love him. But men like him do not
have such pleasant things. Their constant preoccupation with
their art keeps them from being gracious and neat and even
makes them unpolished in spite of their intelligence.'
Honoré de Balzac, about 1845, by Louis Auguste Bisson.

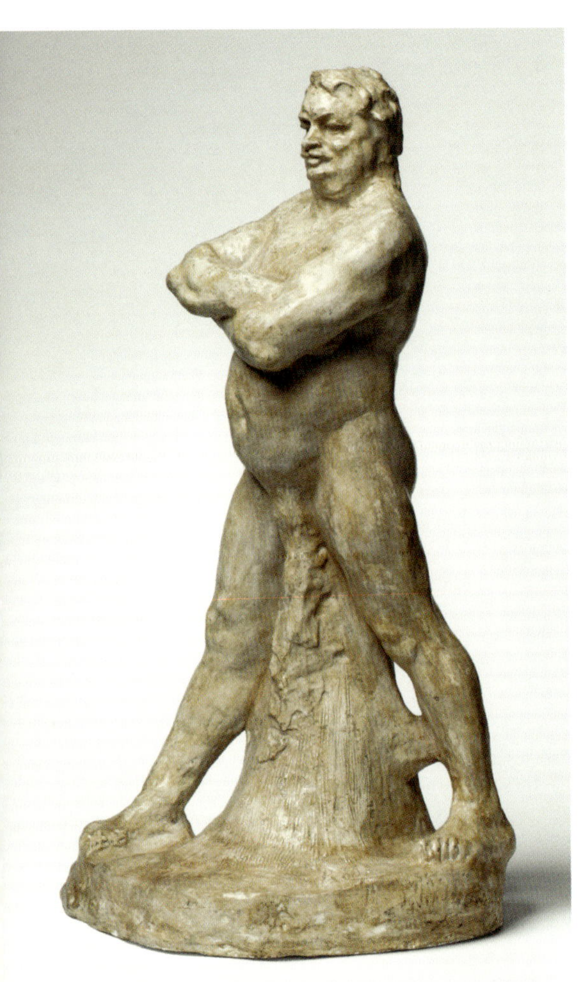

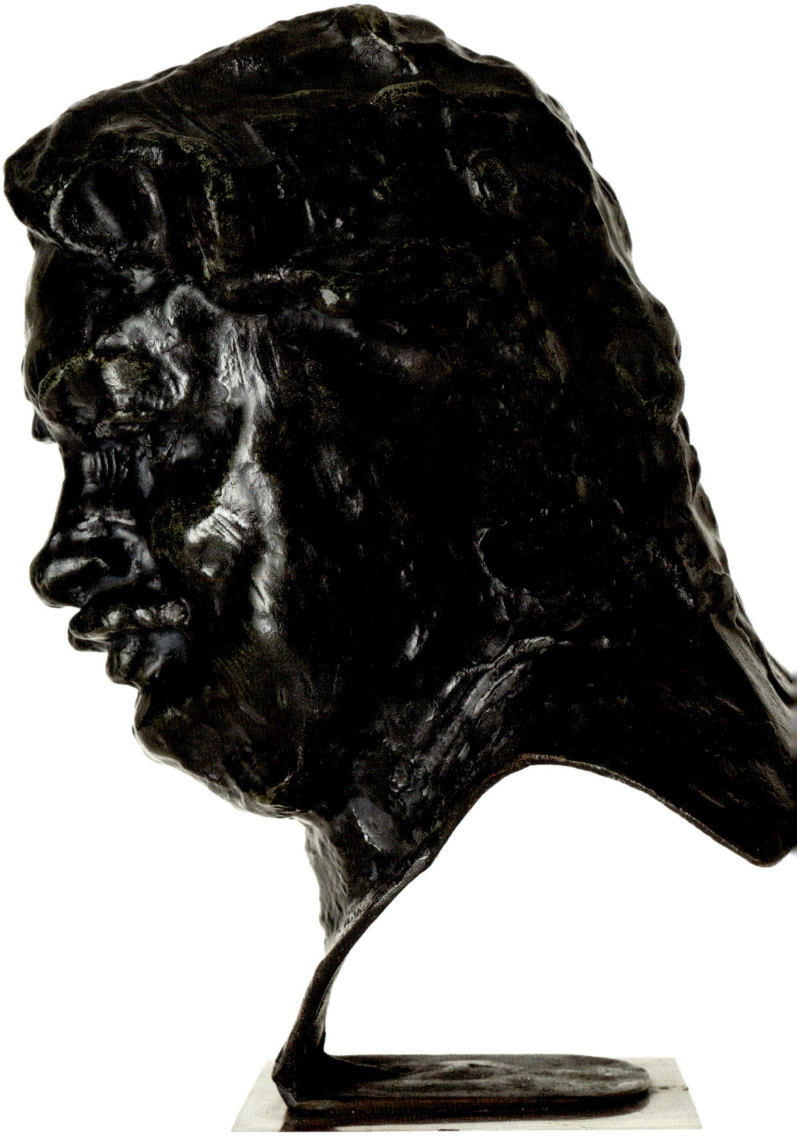

When working on a figure that required clothing, Rodin customarily sculpted a naked figure first. This allowed him to fully model bodies, before adding clothes later. The bust of Balzac in the Burrell Collection was created from this full-length nude sculpture of Balzac. *Naked Balzac*, about 1892–93, by Auguste Rodin, plaster, painted with varnish. Philadelphia Museum of Art, 1971-143-1.

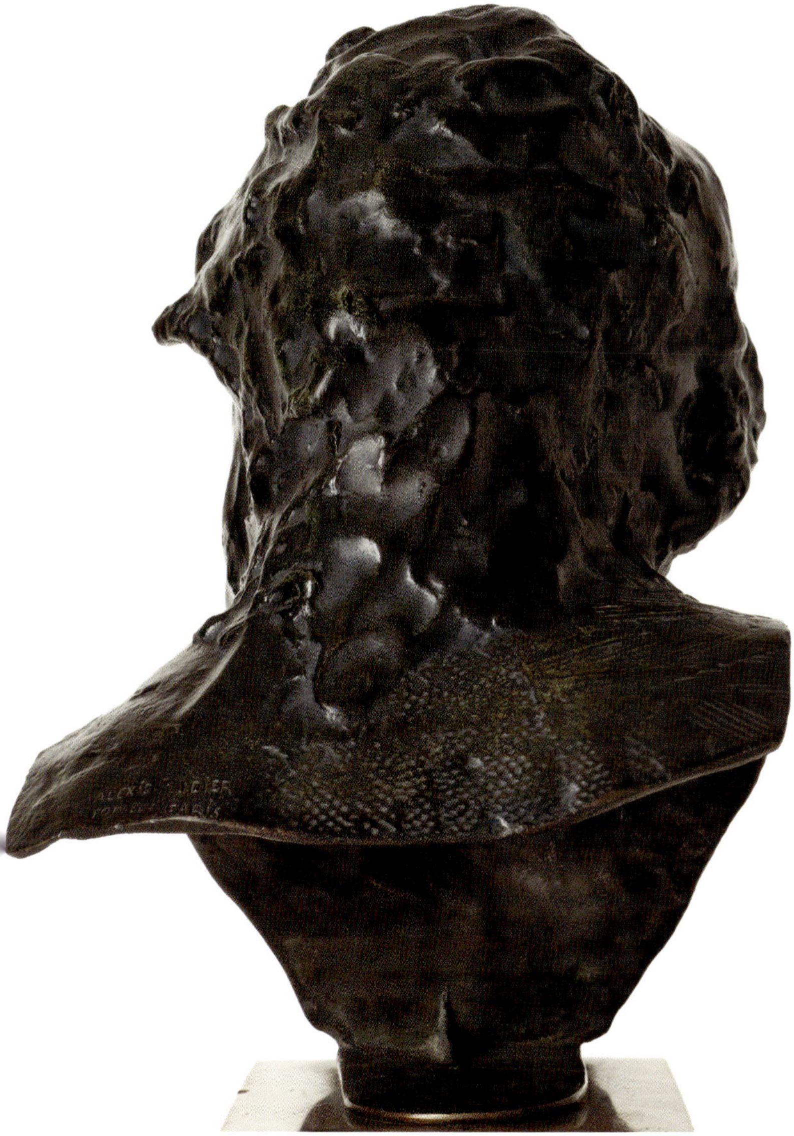

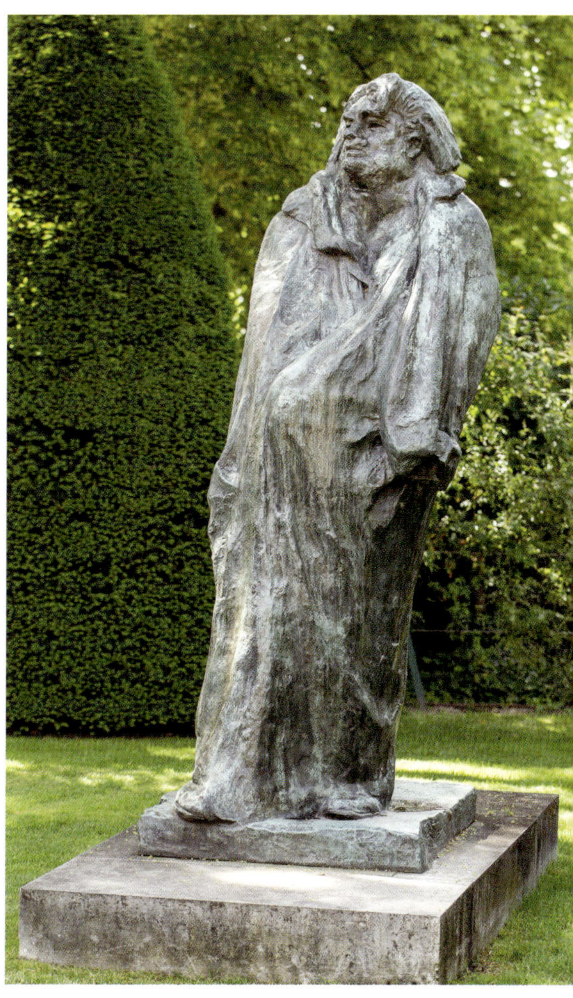

For the head of his final design, Rodin found a model with more pronounced facial features than the model for the full-length nude study of Balzac. When it was eventually revealed in 1898, *Balzac* was swiftly rejected. Critics likened the sculpture to a seal, a bag of cement or even a snowman. *Balzac*, 1898, by Auguste Rodin, bronze. Musée Rodin, Paris, s.1294.

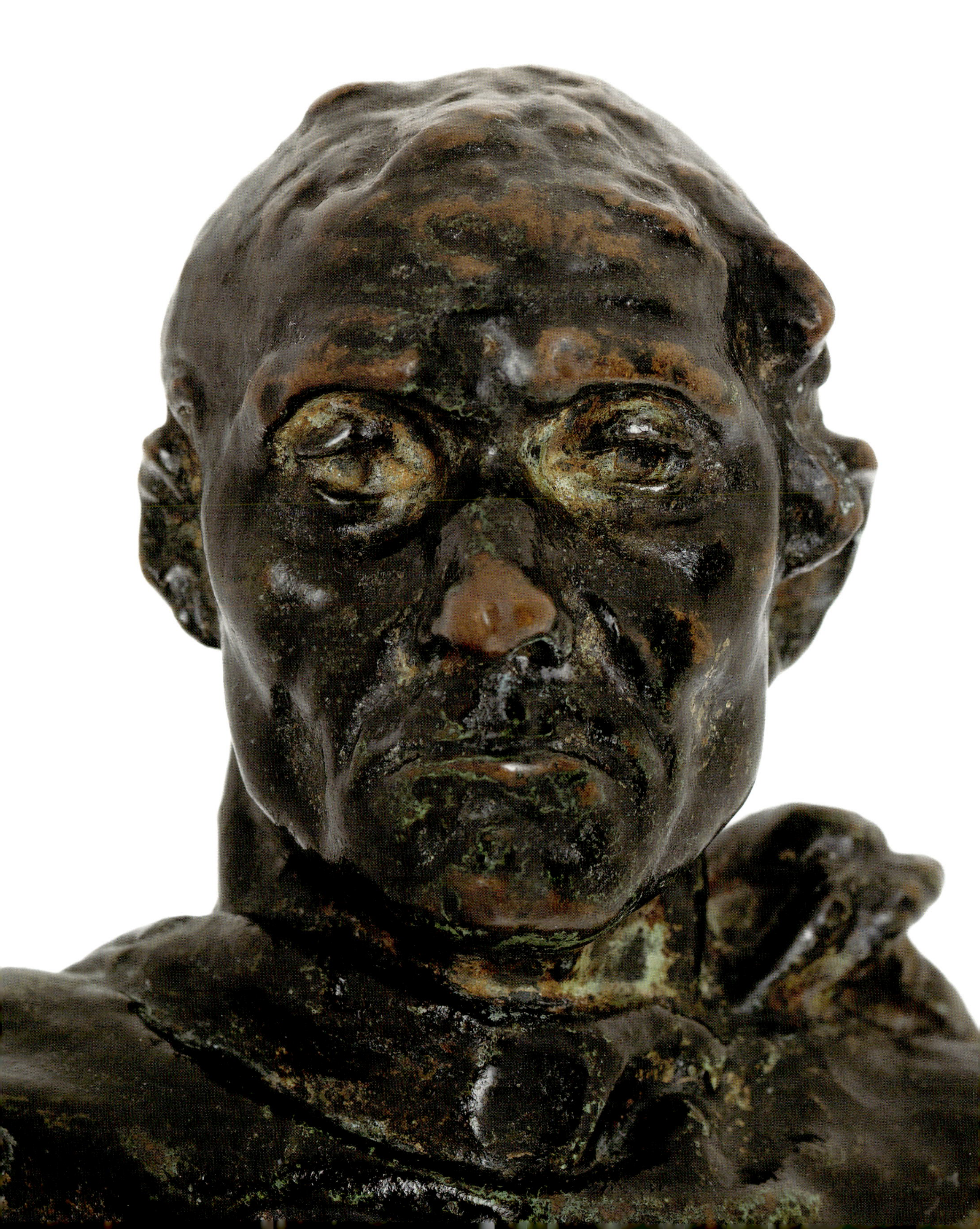

Jean d'Aire, Burgher of Calais, 1895

Cast in bronze by Alexis Rudier Foundry, 1903–17
Bronze
46.7 x 16.3 x 15.4 cm
7.14

The figure of Jean d'Aire is part of a group sculpture which Rodin was commissioned to make in 1885. The monument commemorates the bravery shown by six burghers – leading citizens – in 1347, at the end of the siege of their city during the Hundred Years War. When Calais surrendered to King Edward III of England (1312–77), he demanded, for the wider population to be spared, that six prominent citizens offer to surrender to him and, with nooses around their necks, bring out the keys to the city. In the events that followed, the expected execution of the men did not take place, but their willingness to sacrifice their lives for their fellow citizens is still remembered. In Rodin's sculpture, Jean d'Aire is clutching the keys to the city, which he is about to hand to the English. His face is set in grim acceptance of his anticipated fate.

The original commission was monumental in size, the six burghers larger than life-sized. Rodin modelled the figures individually, and later arranged for copies of the sculptures to be made at a reduced size and sold as single figures, as the one in the Burrell Collection.

Rodin's sculpture of the six burghers of Calais shows them dressed in loose gowns and with ropes around their necks, ready for execution, with expressions and poses that reveal their internal struggle as they prepare for death. *Monument to the Burghers of Calais*, 1889, by Auguste Rodin, bronze. Victoria Tower Gardens, London.

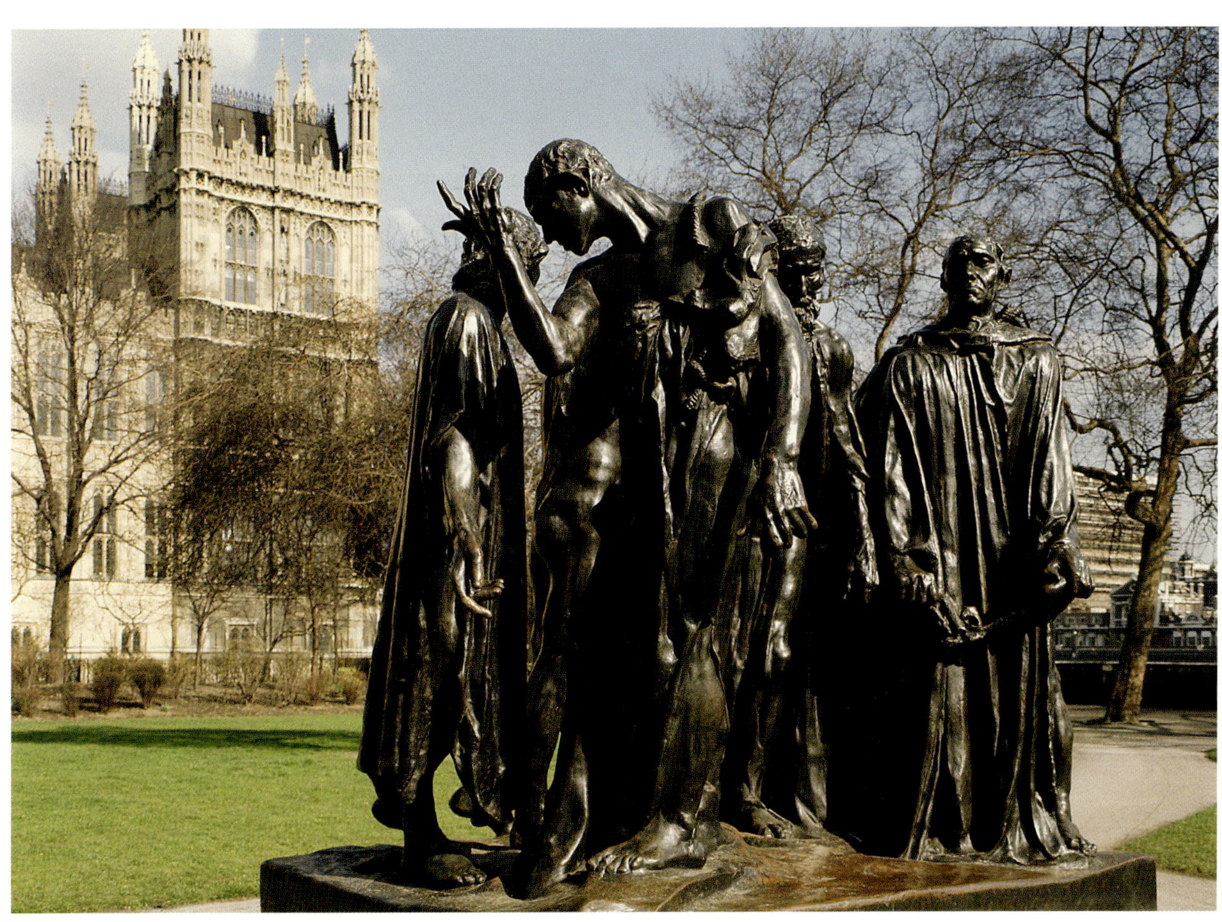

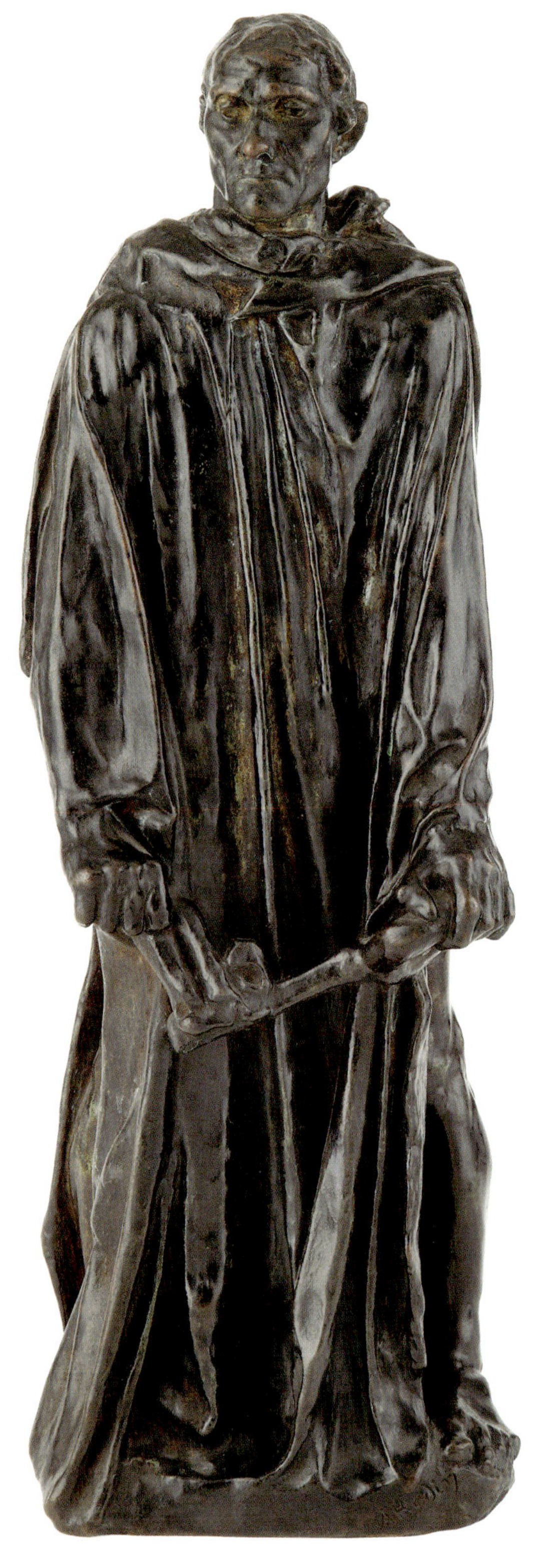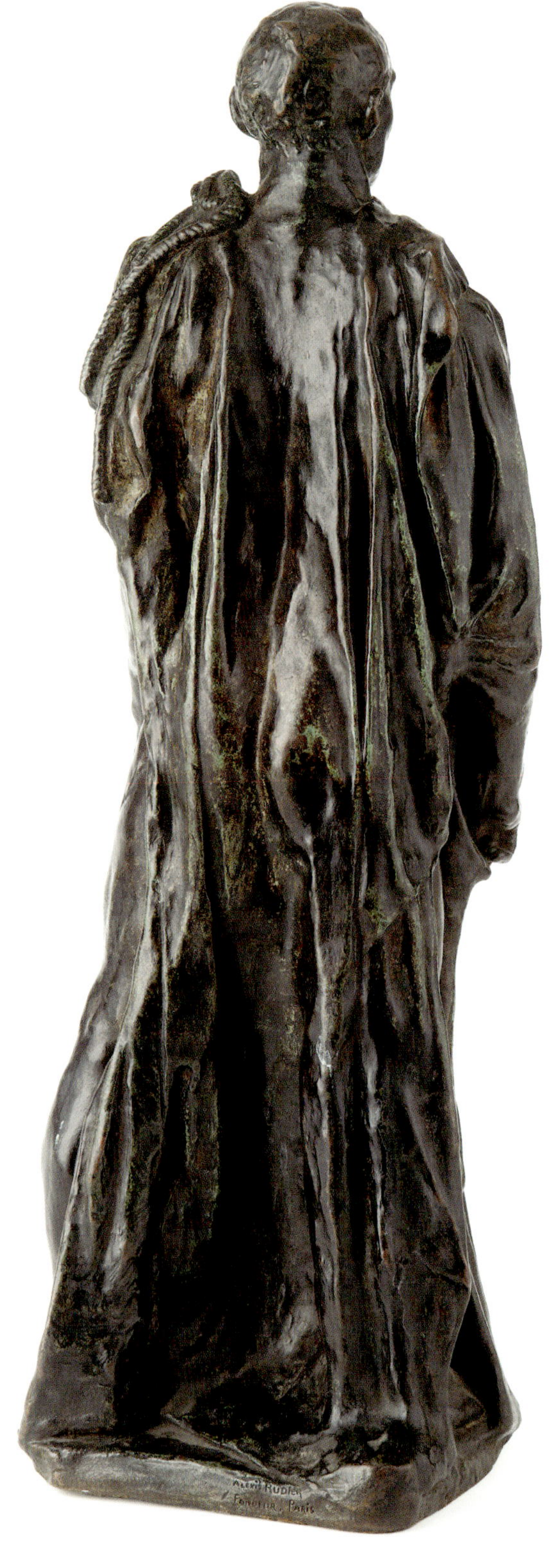

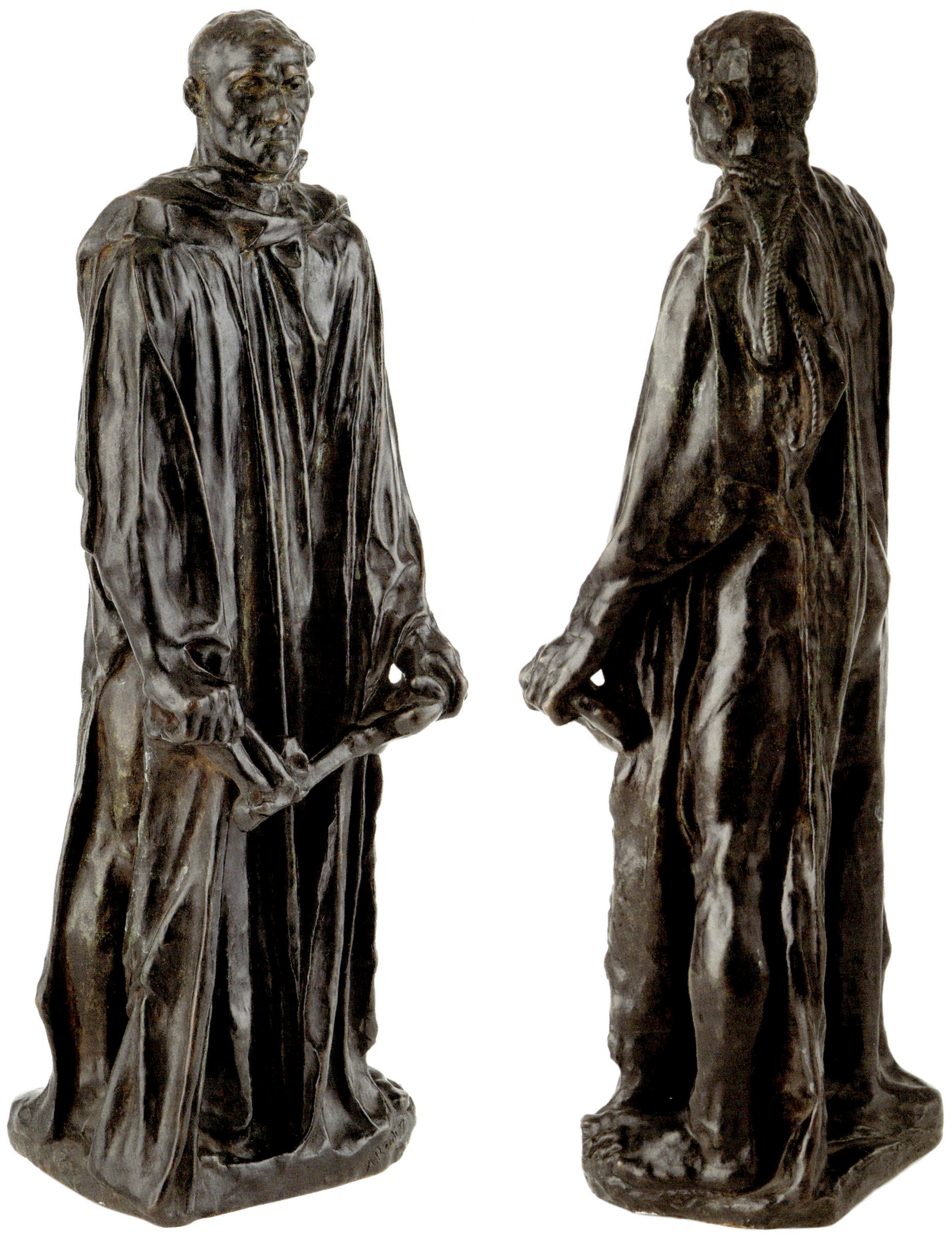

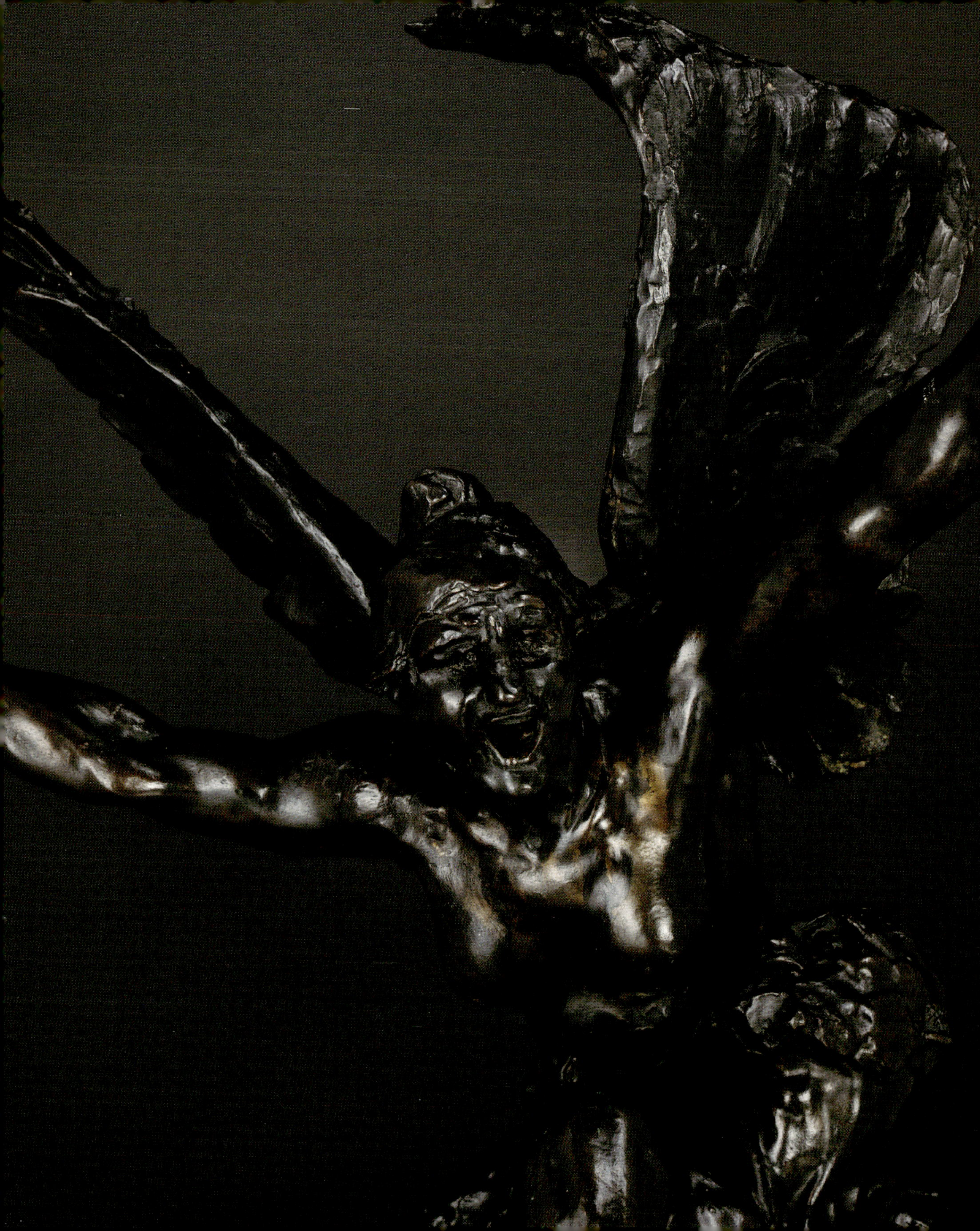

The Call to Arms, 1879
Probably cast in bronze before 1921
Bronze
111 x 58 x 40 cm
7.6

Rodin originally submitted this design as a
competition entry for a monument paying homage
to the many Parisians who died in the bitter struggle
to defend their city during the Franco-Prussian
war of 1870–71. His entry did not get past the first
round. Rodin admitted that it 'must have seemed
too violent, too strident'. The terrifying, screaming
female figure with raised arms is the embodiment
of war, victory and freedom, sometimes called the
'genius of liberty'. With her contorted expression
and open mouth, she seems to be releasing a fierce
battle cry. She supports a dying soldier, who still
clutches a broken sword in his left hand.

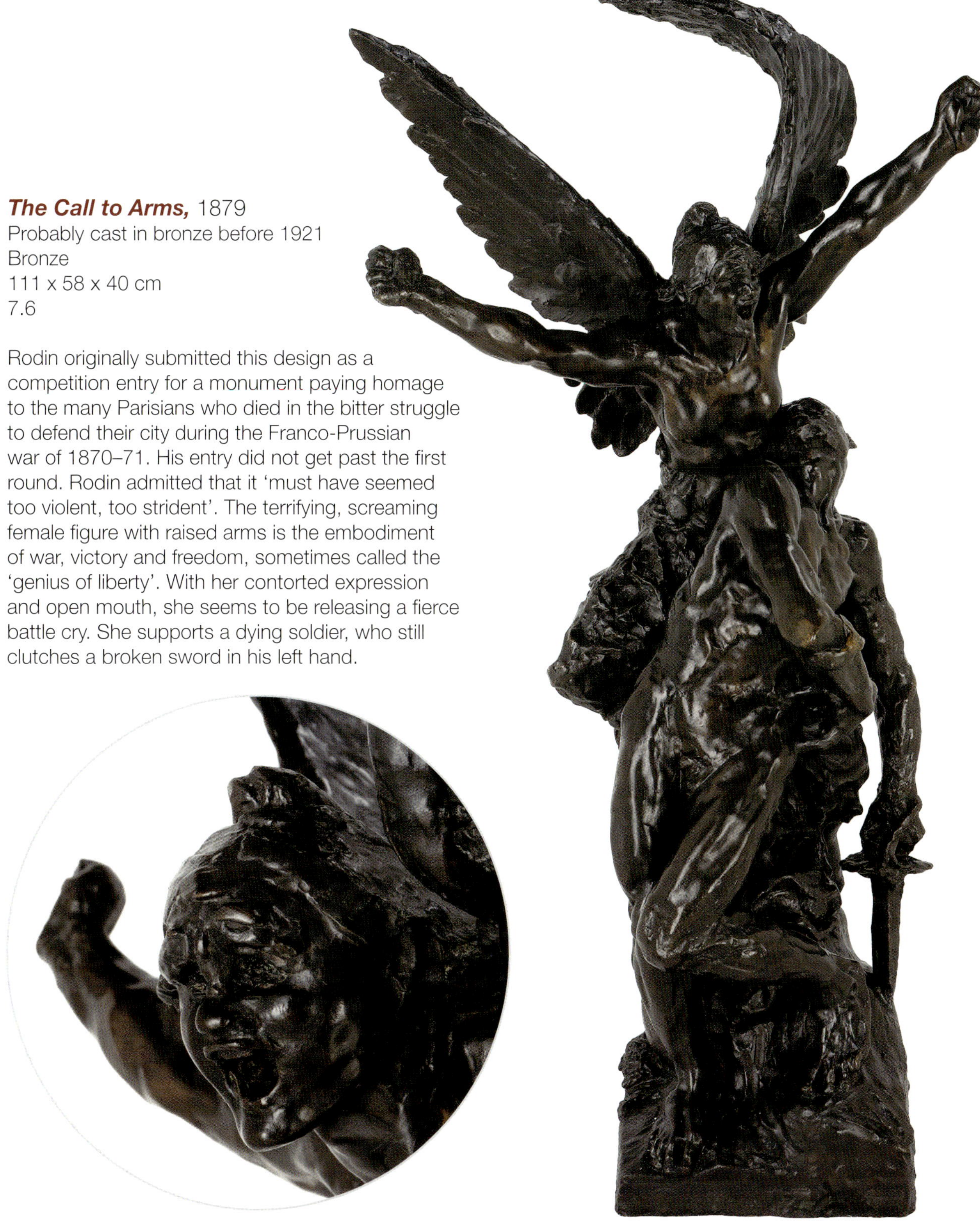

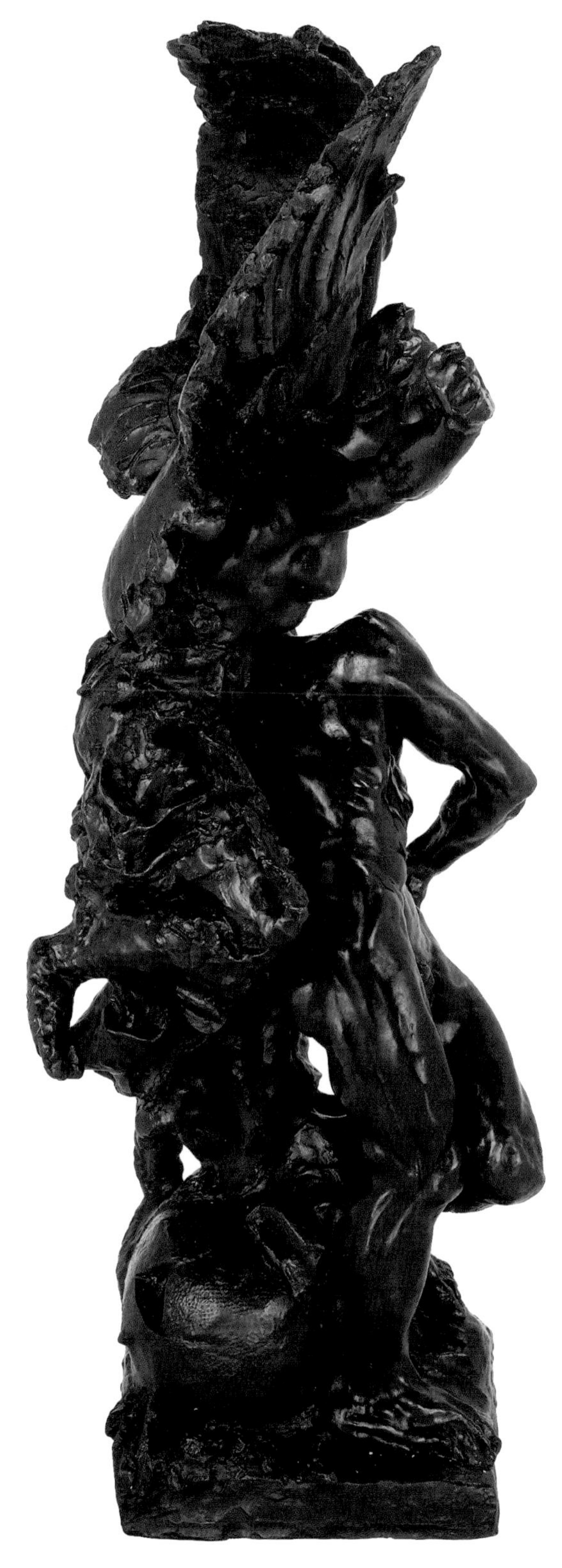

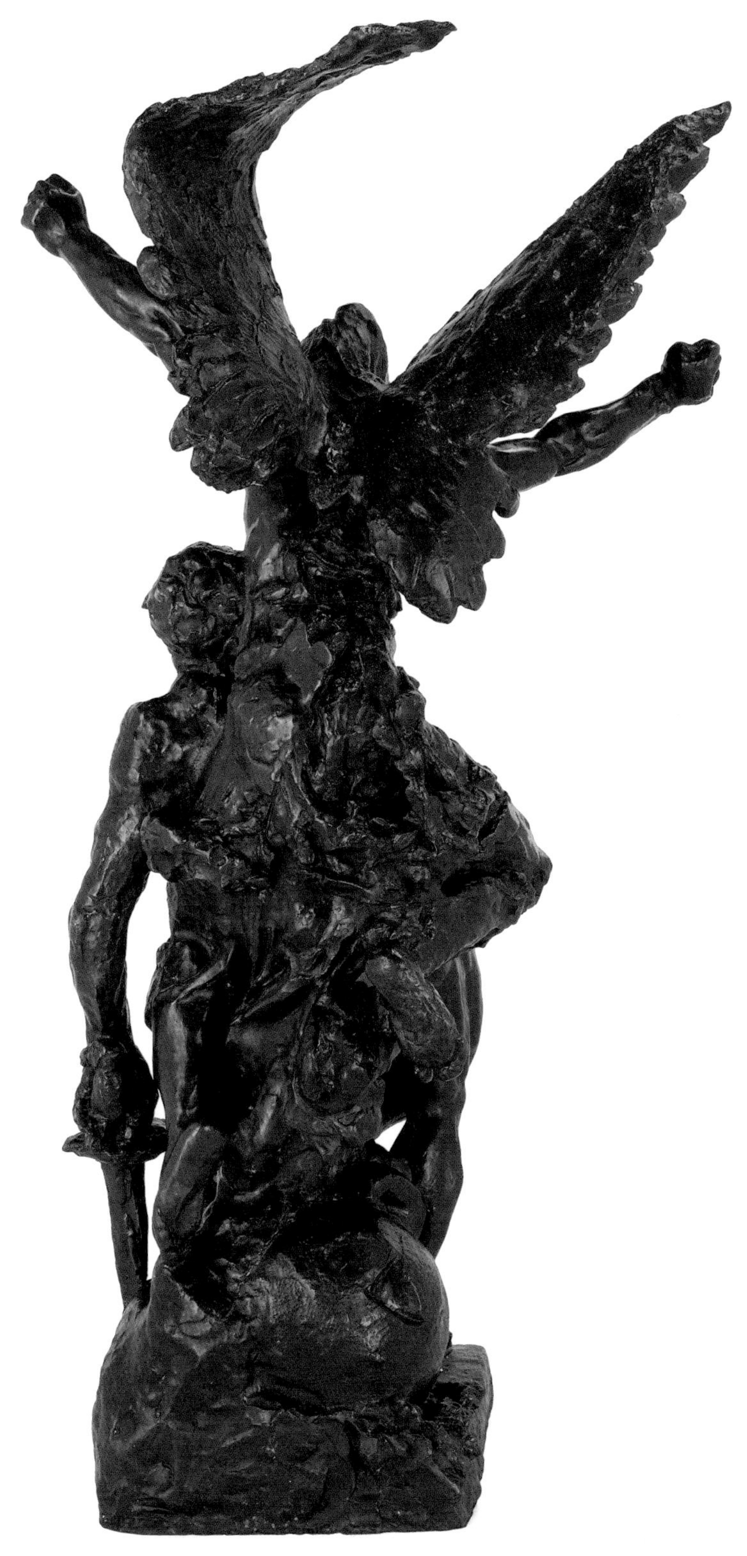

Further Reading

Martin Bellamy and Isobel MacDonald, *William Burrell: A Collector's Life*, Glasgow Museums and Birlinn, Edinburgh, 2022. Biography of William Burrell, his life, collection and legacy.

Ruth Butler, *Rodin: The Shape of Genius*, Yale University Press, London, 1996. Biography of Auguste Rodin which includes descriptions of his most important artworks, as well as looking deeply into life events that influenced the way Rodin worked.

Albert E Elsen, *In Rodin's Studio: A Photographic Record of Sculpture in the Making*, Phaidon, Oxford, 1980. Reproductions of many photographs of Rodin at work in his studio, which allow an insight into the way the great sculptor worked, with explanatory notes.

Catherine Lampert, *Rodin: Sculpture and Drawings*, Arts Council of Great Britain, London, 1986. Published to accompany a major exhibition at Hayward Gallery, London (1 November 1986–25 January 1987), this catalogue looks closely at some of Rodin's major projects and explores the relationship between Rodin's sculpture and drawing.

Antoinette le Normand-Romain, *The Bronzes of Rodin: Catalogue of Works in the Musée Rodin (Volumes I and II)*, Musée Rodin and Éditions de la Réunion des Musées Nationaux, Paris, 2007. Comprehensive double-volume catalogue of Rodin's bronzes in the Musée Rodin, Paris, which also lists all the other known casts of each sculpture, details casting techniques and gives an introduction to Rodin's bronzes.

Antoinette le Normand-Romain, *Camille Claudel and Rodin: Time will Heal Everything*, Musée Rodin and Hermann, Paris, 2014. Introductory book examining the relationship between Claudel and Rodin.

John L Tancock, *The Sculpture of Auguste Rodin: The Collection of the Rodin Museum, Philadelphia*, Philadelphia Museum of Art, 1976. The impressive collection of works in the Rodin Museum, Philadelphia, is examined in categories such as Portraits, The Gates of Hell and Small Groups and Figures: a useful guide to some of the most important works by Rodin.